C000126550

Living in the House of God

Monastic Essays

A gift from the
Simon Mapp
Awards

www.simonmappawards.com

MONASTIC WISDOM SERIES

Simeon Leiva, OCSO, General Editor

Advisory Board

Michael Casey, OCSO

Lawrence S. Cunningham

Patrick Hart, OCSO

Robert Heller

Terrence Kardong, OSB

Kathleen Norris

Miriam Pollard, OCSO

Bonnie Thurston

MONASTIC WISDOM SERIES: NUMBER THIRTY-TWO

Living in the House of God

Monastic Essays

by

Margaret Malone, SGS

Foreword by
Michael Casey, OCSO

Cistercian Publications
www.cistercianpublications.org

LITURGICAL PRESS
Collegeville, Minnesota
www.litpress.org

A Cistercian Publications title published by Liturgical Press

Cistercian Publications
Editorial Offices
161 Grosvenor Street
Athens, Ohio 54701
www.cistercianpublications.org

Unless otherwise indicated, Vatican documents quoted in this work are taken from the Vatican website.

Unless otherwise indicated, Scripture texts in this work are taken from the *New Revised Standard Version Bible,* © 1989, Division of Christian Education of the National Council of the Churches of Christ in the United States of America. Used by permission. All rights reserved.

Excerpt from the English translation of the *The Roman Missal* © 2010, International Commission on English in the Liturgy Corporation. All rights reserved.

© 2014 by Order of Saint Benedict, Collegeville, Minnesota. All rights reserved. No part of this book may be reproduced in any form, by print, microfilm, microfiche, mechanical recording, photocopying, translation, or any other means, known or yet unknown, for any purpose except brief quotations in reviews, without the previous written permission of Liturgical Press, Saint John's Abbey, PO Box 7500, Collegeville, Minnesota 56321-7500. Printed in the United States of America.

1	2	3	4	5	6	7	8	9

Library of Congress Cataloging-in-Publication Data

Malone, Margaret, SGS.
   [Essays. Selections]
   Living in the house of God : monastic essays / by Margaret Malone, SGS ; foreword by Michael Casey, OCSO.
      pages   cm. — (Monastic wisdom series ; no. 32)
   ISBN 978-0-87907-032-8 — ISBN 978-0-87907-716-7 (ebook)
   1. Benedictines—Spiritual life.   I. Title.

BX3003.M285   2014
255'.1—dc23   2014020398

Contents

Foreword

A FEW YEARS AGO I READ AN ARTICLE IN AN airline magazine in which the author insisted that different styles of wines must be served in glasses especially designed to enhance their specific qualities. A person who drinks shiraz from a glass designed for pinot noir may be considered to lack finesse. I suppose the author knew what he was talking about. What I chose to hear him saying was that the objective quality of a wine is filtered through various components on the receiving end, such as the shape of the glass, and that these extrinsic factors change the experience of drinking it. In general this seems to be true, since we all recognize that a good wine is often enhanced by the food it accompanies, and drinking it with friends in a pleasant ambience makes it even better. The enjoyment of a wine is more than can be measured by scientific analysis. Subjective influences add value to the finished product.

In a similar way, the fact that ancient texts are received into different subjective environments means that the tradition they embody is modified according to the condition of those who receive it. There is more in such texts than their authors supposed. On the basis of their own very different circumstances, those who read the Rule of Saint Benedict appreciate different aspects of its teaching—sometimes perceiving elements that were concealed even from its author. It is in this way that tradition reinvigorates itself by proclaiming its message in different contexts. We can go further. Tradition is not only subject to adaptation in order that it might become comprehensible to people in different cultures but also is itself enriched in the process of being inculturated.

Beyond the necessity of scholarly examination that rigorously establishes a likely original meaning of the Rule, there is also scope for a complementary reflection that seeks to bring the beliefs and values of the Rule into dialogue with contemporary experience, insights, and aspirations. Academic work tends to narrow the possibilities so that conclusions are arrived at with some degree of certainty. The more humane study of the texts builds on this scholarly foundation to relocate the Rule in different contexts, to receive the message with a different sensitivity and, perhaps, to perceive previously unheard echoes, sometimes in unlikely places.

A twenty-first-century person reads the Rule in a manner different from someone in the nineteenth century. A nonmonastic reader may be conscious of nuances that monks and nuns miss. Probably a female reader catches assonances that may escape her male counterpart. A practical person delights in sections of the Rule that pass unnoticed by the theoretician. In fact each person receives the Rule in a unique way. Each of us arrives at a personal accommodation with the text of the Rule and the tradition which it engendered. This is why it is enriching to discuss the meaning of the Rule with persons of different backgrounds, or to read commentaries that reflect the personal circumstances of the author. It is not so much a question of deciding who has the "right" interpretation of the Rule but of opening oneself to wonder at how the Rule can communicate such a variety of complementary messages without loss of its own integrity.

Margaret Malone is a Sister of the Good Samaritan of the Order of Saint Benedict, a congregation of sisters founded in Australia in the nineteenth century by Archbishop John Bede Polding, OSB. For more than half a century she has been involved in education at every level, equipping herself along the way with an impressive set of academic credentials culminating in her doctorate from the Australian National University on the Benedictine approach to authority. She is an engaging and insightful lecturer on monastic topics who is as much appreciated for her warmth and humanity as for her ability to bring the traditional themes of monastic spirituality into conversation with contemporary culture.

Sister Margaret's involvement with Benedictine studies stems from the period immediately following the Second Vatican Council, when the Sisters of the Good Samaritan were engaged in the work of renewal and seeking to clarify their origins. The question they asked concerned the applicability of a sixth-century monastic rule to the lives of women in a congregation founded in colonial Australia and engaged in a range of active apostolates. There were only two real possibilities. One was to abandon the Benedictine component in their identity and redefine themselves in terms of apostolic religious life. The other was to go beyond the external structures of nineteenth-century Benedictinism to arrive at an understanding of the underlying beliefs and values of the Benedictine Rule and apply these to the present life of the congregation. That the congregation chose the latter option is due in no small measure to its willingness to study the Rule and provide access for its members to the fruits of contemporary scholarship. Sister Margaret was one of those who have been involved for more than three decades in demonstrating the flexibility of the Benedictine tradition and exploring its relevance to areas of contemporary concern.

The chapters in this book all originated in talks given by the author in various places. They were then, in most cases, revised and published. Inevitably the different articles bear the imprint of the audience to which they were first addressed, but they belong together as different expressions of a fundamental attitude to the Rule—one that is not only strongly ecclesial and sacramental but also firmly linked to the realities of everyday fidelity.

I had read most of these articles previously but, upon rereading them, I noted how well the various essays fit together and the high degree of consistency they demonstrated even though they approached the Rule from different angles. Many of the linkages made in these reflections are engagingly original, reflecting the author's particular situation and context. They clearly derived from lived experience and from years of teaching. The essays are written in a simple expository style that is accessible to almost anyone who will pick up the book, yet there is a depth and honesty about them that will motivate readers not only to keep reading but also to think more profoundly about some of the issues raised. Together they embody a coherent vision of the Rule that has grown in the heart of the author through many decades of living and teaching it.

Just as there are many factors involved when good wine sings sweetly to the palate of the drinker, there are many elements in the enjoyment of a book that aims at making an ancient text part of a modern conversation. In the case of *Living in the House of God*, diligent background reading has provided a firm foundation for free-flowing reflections on a variety of topics that open up areas of the Rule that have been, for many potential readers, previously unexplored. Much work has gone into the planning of these essays, yet they are presented in a friendly way that is not likely to frighten away those who would feel out of their depths in a more technical discussion. There is much here that will give the reader pause for thought. At the end of the book not a few will feel that the beverage offered by Sister Margaret is definitely a sparkling wine.

Michael Casey, OCSO
Tarrawarra Abbey, Australia

Editor's Note

THE NEW REVISED STANDARD VERSION OF the Bible has been used throughout, except when the passage of Scripture in question is being quoted directly from a passage in the Rule of Saint Benedict. For the Rule of Saint Benedict, two translations have been used: *RB 1980: The Rule of St. Benedict in Latin and English with Notes,* ed. Timothy Fry (Collegeville, MN: Liturgical Press, 1981), and Terrence Kardong, *Benedict's Rule: A Translation and Commentary* (Collegeville, MN: Liturgical Press, 1996).

1

Living in the House of God

A BUILDING, A HOUSE CAN JUST BE a shell. A house derives its meaning from those who live or work therein and from the way they interact. If we are to call our house a house of God we must make it so by the way we live. We pray in Psalm 27: "One thing I asked of the LORD, that I will seek after: to live in the house of the LORD all the days of my life" (Ps 27:4). So how should we live in this house of God? We know that the way a building is shaped also helps in determining the way those within it live and relate. We are indeed formed by what we form. Qualities such as integrity, hospitality, humanity, and beauty in a place will enable its dwellers to live lives in which such qualities are evident. The way we understand who we are and how we live will be reflected in our places and vice versa. Our places become bearers of meaning and memory.

In one of his conferences, Cassian makes this very point:

> Piamun: Although some people are in the habit of speaking of monasteries instead of cenobia, without drawing a distinction, nonetheless the difference is that "monastery" is the name of a dwelling and means nothing more than a place—that is, a lodging for monks—whereas "cenobium" indicates the character and discipline of the profession itself. The habitation of even one monk can be called a monastery, but something cannot be called

a cenobium unless a united community with several inhabitants lives there.[1]

Without making a dichotomy between the place itself and what is done within it, I would like to explore the connections.

Elizabeth Jolly, a Western Australian writer, when writing about the monastic town of New Norcia and its sense of place, quoted a comment made to her by E. J. Stormon, SJ, who had collected the memoirs of Salvado, the founder of New Norcia Monastery. When speaking to her about a visit she was to make there, Stormon said: "Landscapes have their voices."[2] So, too, do buildings, homes, houses, and monasteries. They speak with their voices and our voices about our lives. One of the founders of Cîteaux, Saint Stephen Harding, was said to be "a lover of the Rule and of the place."

It is interesting that in liturgical documents much emphasis is given to the importance of space and place in relation to what is done within those spaces.[3] In giving attention to church architecture, the basic questions that should be asked before a building is constructed are questions such as these: "Who are the people who use this building?" "What do we do together in it?" and then, "What environment do we need?" There is no doubt that, while what is done by the people in

---

[1] John Cassian, *Conference* 18.10, in *John Cassian: The Conferences*, trans. Boniface Ramsey (New York: Paulist Press, 1997), 643.

[2] David Hutchinson, ed., *A Town Like No Other: The Living Tradition of New Norcia* (Fremantle, Australia: Fremantle Arts Centre Press, 1995), 56.

[3] Such documents include: "Environment and Art in Catholic Worship," in *The Liturgy Documents: A Parish Resource*, 3rd ed. (Chicago: Liturgy Training Publications, 1991); "The Place of Worship," Irish Episcopal Commission for Liturgy (Dublin, 1994); "Built of Living Stones: Art, Architecture, and Worship," U.S. Conference of Catholic Bishops (Washington, DC, 2000); and "Our Place of Worship," Canadian Conference of Catholic Bishops (Ottawa, 2000).

the building is crucial, attention must be given to the building itself, because it in turn will affect those who inhabit and use it.

The document on "Environment and Art in Catholic Worship" makes an interesting point:

> When the Christian community gathers to celebrate its faith and vision, it gathers to celebrate what is most personally theirs and most nobly human and truly Church. The actions of the assembly witness the great deed God has done; they confirm an age-old covenant. With such vision and depth of the assembly, can the environment be anything less than a vehicle to meet the Lord and encounter one another? The challenge to our environment is the final challenge of Christ. We must make ready until he returns in glory.[4]

And another relevant text stresses the importance of the environment and the interaction with those who inhabit it: "The environment is appropriate when it is beautiful, when it is hospitable, when it clearly invites and needs an assembly of people to complete it."[5] Surely both these texts could also apply to Benedict's house of God and those who dwell therein.

Throughout history, the buildings of those who lived religious lives did indeed reflect the lives of those who dwelt there, seeking God. History also tells us that when the community was in decline for whatever reason, the buildings decayed and the ruins of many monasteries give testimony to this. As long as the lives of the community flourished, however, the buildings illustrated the stability of the community. Stability did not mean a community that was static and lifeless. The places for prayer, for living together and apart, and

---

[4] "Environment and Art in Catholic Worship," in *The Liturgy Documents: A Parish Resource,* 3rd ed. (Chicago: Liturgy Training Publications, 1991), par. 107, p. 338.

[5] "Environment and Art in Catholic Worship," in *Liturgy Documents,* par. 24, p. 323.

for work and rest were designed appropriately and spoke of a regular and stable lifestyle grounded in solid understandings. The words of Jacob after he awoke from his dream apply here: "How awesome is this place! This is none other than the house of God and this is the gate of heaven" (Gen 28:17). In the dream God had promised that, although Jacob's offspring would be spread abroad all over the earth, God would always be with him: "Know that I am with you and will keep you wherever you go, and will bring you back to this land; for I will not leave you until I have done what I have promised you" (Gen 28:15). Whether Jacob knew it or not, God was always with him in "this place."

"House of God" or *Domus Dei* is a term used three times by Benedict. Whether explicitly or implicitly, the idea is important because of what it conveys, not only about the building, the monastery, but also about the life of the cenobium, the community who live in the monastery. When Benedict gives a definition of "cenobites," he explains that the cenobites are those who belong to a monastery, where they serve under a rule and an abbot (1.2).[6] Benedict envisages that the monastery should be so constructed that within it are all the necessities for living the life to which they have dedicated themselves. He feared that, if monks were "to roam outside," it would not be good for their souls: "The monastery should, if possible, be so constructed that within it all necessities, such as water, mill and garden, are contained, and the various crafts are practiced" (66.6).

The three occasions when Benedict uses the phrase *Domus Dei* all reflect his concern that in this "house of God" there be an ordered life, one that provides a structure that facilitates the seeking of God by the community members and the stable environment needed.

---

[6] References to the Rule of St. Benedict are given in parentheses after a quotation or paraphrase by simply noting chapter and verse. In this case "(1.2)" means "Rule of St. Benedict, chapter 1, verse 2."

The first time the phrase is used is in chapter 31, "Qualifications of the Monastery Cellarer." In the context of how the goods of the monastery are cared for, Benedict reminds the monks that there is a right time for things to be done: "Necessary items are to be requested and given at the proper times, so that no one may be disquieted or distressed in the house of God" (31.18-19).

In the chapter "On the Reception of Guests," which is concerned that the guest be truly received as Christ, there are practical arrangements described that should reflect this concern: suitable kitchen arrangements, help given to the guestmaster when needed, the provision of adequate bedding, and then the very important prescription that the guest quarters are to be entrusted to a God-fearing brother: "The house of God should be in the care of wise men who will manage it wisely" (53.22). The repetition of the idea of *wisdom—Et domus Dei a* sapientibus *et* sapienter *administretur*—emphasizes the importance, not simply of an ordered household but also of the relationships that those who act wisely engender.

The third use of the term occurs in chapter 64, "On the Election of an Abbot." There is an overall concern for the abbot to be a worthy steward, not one who would go along with any evil ways of the community. What must happen is that those who block any wicked conspiracy in this direction must "set a worthy steward in charge of God's house" (64.5). In the context of Benedict's detailed teaching on the abbot, it is obvious that being a worthy steward embraces both care of the goods and care of the people who make up the community. Stewardship of the community is an overarching responsibility, so that all is ordered and well in the house of God.

It is interesting to explore the significance of the places in the monastery that are given special attention by Benedict. Some of these are the gate, the place for the novices, the room of gathering for discussion—the chapter room—the oratory, the kitchen and the places for eating, where the monks sleep, the place for guests, the room of the porter, the place where the sick are cared for, and the place for the storage of tools and goods. All of these are significant because of the purpose they serve. I will now consider some of these uses and connections.

At the Gates

The first significant place of the monastery is the gate or the entrance or door. To this place come those who wish to join the community of their own choice or the young who are offered by parents, visiting monks and priests who wish to stay, guests who visit for a shorter or longer time, and those who come to ask for help or bring a message. The monks who belong to the community but who have to travel for any reason or who work far away from the monastery also return through the gate or entrance. Brothers who leave the monastery at "the devil's suggestion" will leave through the entrance where they had spent time in the past, persevering until they were accepted.

Having entered the "gate" of the Christian life through baptism, some feel the desire and the call to live their baptismal life as members of a community, where they will live in a monastery serving under a rule and an abbot (1.2). This first gate of the monastery does not open easily for the newcomers. There is need for perseverance in knocking and asking for entrance—a sort of indication that what is desired demands earnest commitment. The ones seeking admittance to the community must continue knocking without any reply and keep on bearing this harsh treatment patiently for four or five days. This is indeed a test to discover whether those knocking are serious in their desire. When they are admitted, they do not gain open access to the community or the life of the monks. They are required to stay in the guest quarters, and then eventually they are able to live in the novitiate, where they are given careful attention and are "clearly told all the hardships and difficulties that will lead [them] to God" (58.1-8).

After various phases of learning about the Rule and the life he desires to live, the newcomer is received in the oratory in the presence of the whole community. Thus the oratory is central to his admission. And within this oratory is another significant place—the altar on which he lays with his own hand the document that contains his promise of stability, fidelity to monastic life, and obedience. Having sung the *Suscipe* and asked the prayers of each monk, he has passed through another gate and "from that very day he is to be counted as one of the community" (58.20-23). In the case of the offering of sons who are too young to do all of this, the document and the boy's hand are wrapped in the cloth of the altar (59.2). So powerful a symbol of the monk's offering is this altar on which the document is laid that Benedict states that, if the monk should leave, "that document of his which the abbot took from the altar should not be given back to him but kept in the monastery" (58.29).

The gates of the monastery are also significant for those who come as guests, and here entrance is granted much more readily. They are welcomed eagerly as Christ, whatever their status or reason for coming. They are met by the abbot and the whole community with all the courtesy of love. Christ is adored in them: their hands and feet are washed, they are given every kindness, they have the divine law read to them, food and adequate bedding are provided to them. All is done for them with great care and concern (53).

This wholehearted welcome at the gates is also emphasized in the description of the porter, the keeper of the gate. There will always be someone there to give the welcome: "The porter will need a room near the entrance so that visitors will always find him there to answer them" (66.2). He answers the call with all gentleness and with the warmth of love (66.4), and help is given as required. Others who come and wish to stay as guests are given a ready welcome as has been described.

Within the Gates

Within the monastery itself the places are arranged and spoken of in a way that shows how important they are to the life of the community. One of the most significant places is the oratory. Its role in relation to the newcomer's reception into the community has already been described. Benedict also devotes chapter 52 to the oratory. In this chapter the emphasis is on the role of the place in relation to what is done there—the prayer of the community. In one of those pithy statements with which he often commences his chapters, Benedict states: "The oratory ought to be what it is called, and nothing else is to be done or stored there" (52.1). It is assumed that the Work of God is celebrated there, and Benedict does not enlarge on that in this place, except to state that after the Work of God all should leave in silence and reverence so that those who wish to stay there and pray should be undisturbed (52.2-3). The oratory is also a place where the members of the community may go and pray privately at other times, and here Benedict describes some of the attitudes to prayer that will be part of that prayer: compunction, prayer with tears, and *intentio cordis*, that is, prayer with great attention and longing and reaching out for God. Nothing should get in the way of anyone's desire to pray like this, and the oratory provides a place which is silent and undisturbed for this expression of one's seeking of God.

Benedict would no doubt agree with a comment by Dr. Ken Davidson when speaking of his experience of inspiration, grace, and the "elegant solution":

> There has been a long-held view in many cultures that being in sacred places enhances the experience of grace— they are seen as "thin" places where the separation between the material and divine is minimal. To me this means that we should preserve and foster such places— limit the use of churches to spiritual activities and not turn them into "multi-purpose" halls; and set aside at home places which we use only for our devotions.[7]

---

[7] Ken Davidson, "Inspiration and the Elegant Solution: Grace in Secular Life," *Tjurunga 75* (November, 2008): 60.

The centrality of the oratory is also highlighted by the fact that, when the erring monk is to be punished, this involves exclusion from roles in the oratory or, in the case of serious faults, exclusion from the oratory itself. In the case of less serious faults, when he is excluded from the table, he cannot lead a psalm or refrain nor recite a reading in the oratory. Serious as this prohibition is, even worse is the absolute exclusion from the oratory. This symbolizes being cut off from all interactions with the community—working alone, eating alone, no blessings, no communications with anyone. For those who love the community this is a terrible punishment, as illustrated throughout chapters 24 and 25.

Then, as one would expect, it is in the oratory that forgiveness and reconciliation with the community finally happens. It is here that the ritual reintegration of the erring and now repentant monk happens. This involves a gradual reentry: first he lies at the feet of all as they leave the oratory, then at the feet of the abbot and at the feet of all within the oratory, finally returning to a place assigned, though not his own customary place. During this time the monk still cannot lead a psalm or read publicly until final satisfaction has been made. All of this is a powerful ritual enacted in the central place which is the oratory, and it reminds us of the ritual of the return to the Church on Holy Thursday of the sinner who had been excluded.

With echoes of eucharistic theology and its emphasis on table and word, another significant place in the life of the monk is the place where the monk eats and serves. The table in the community is also the place connected with exclusion; from it the monk is excluded for certain faults. Benedict gives a stark description of the monk who has been excluded from the table: he eats alone, the amount of food and the time of the meal are those considered appropriate by the abbot, and the food he eats cannot be blessed (25.5).

It is in chapter 35, "On the Kitchen Servers of the Week," however, that we hear even clearer teaching on the place of the table, the kitchen, and the refectory in the community's life. It is this chapter that describes so many important elements of the community's life, for it is in the context of meals that the brothers serve one another in love, and through such service reward is increased and love fostered (35.1-2, 6). The powerful symbol of the washing of the feet of the monks both before and after their time of service connects the service in love with that of Jesus at the Last Supper.

All care is given here to the serving monks, who are given extra food and drink before their service so that they may serve their brothers without grumbling or hardship (35.13). Great care is also taken of the utensils and tools of service. This place of service is given another dimension by such efforts, prescribed in order to ensure that the service is done well and by the prayer in the oratory before all at the beginning and end of the service. There is thanksgiving at the end—"Blessed are you, Lord God, who have helped me and comforted me" (Ps 86:17)—and at the beginning there had been a prayer for help: "God come to my assistance; Lord make haste to help me" (Ps 70:2; RB 35.15-18). The latter prayer connects the service in this place with the service offered to God in the oratory at the Work of God since both begin with the same verse (17.3; 18.1).

Combined prayer and service toward the brothers remind us of the elements of hospitality expressed when the guests are received into that significant place of the monastery: the place for the guests. This is a place always open to whoever comes, and we are reminded that monasteries are never without guests (53.16). As well as the elements already mentioned when speaking of the "gate" through which the guests find such easy entry, there is in addition another dimension: namely, that in the very service he gives, the one serving also receives. After the washing he is to recite this verse: "God we have received your mercy in the midst of your temple" (Ps 48:10; RB 53.14).

Another important place in the community is the "separate room designated for the sick" (36.7). In this place the same service is to be shown to those sick as is shown to the monks at the table and the guests who come. They are to be served as Christ; there is to be mutual consideration between the sick and those who care for them; and the abbot plays a key role with them, urging that everything be done for them that will help them return to health.

Though the particular place for gathering is not mentioned, if we take notice of what is to be done when the abbot calls the community together to listen to their counsel, we must assume that this gathering place holds great importance in the monastery. When all gather to hear the abbot explain the business on which he must consult the community, this place becomes a place which symbolizes how authority is to be exercised in the community. Indeed, the abbot must make the final decision. But if the matter is important, he must first have listened to the wisdom of the community who are to give prudent and careful advice. In this place one can believe that the Spirit is truly at work when there is a belief that each person is a bearer of wisdom and when that wisdom is offered in a suitable manner. Then everything relating to the life of the community is settled with foresight and fairness (chap. 3).

Benedict never leaves aside a discussion about the practical things that are part of the community's life. We do not know in what places the goods of the monastery (such things as tools or clothing) are kept; but, considering the care that must be given to them, it is sure to be a very well-organized place. A list of the tools is kept by the abbot; they are cared for during use and collected after use (32.2-3). They are entrusted only to those in whom the abbot has confidence, and any failure to keep the things clean or treat them with respect incurs a punishment (32.1, 4). This is not surprising since Benedict considers that all utensils and goods of the monastery are to be regarded as sacred vessels of the altar (31.10). The wardrobe for clothing is a place where used clothing is stored for the poor and where better underclothing for journeys is also stored (55.9, 12).

The place of rest is another important place, and all the monks are "to sleep in one place" (22.3) or, in the case of a large community, in groups of ten or twenty. There is the suggestion of supervision in this arrangement, but it is expressed as "watchful care" that ensures the monks live in the way they promised. In this chapter 22, Benedict also gives direct teaching about the readiness for the Work of God, since the monks must arise without delay and express by their outward behavior that they are eager for the Work of God. With his usual compassion, Benedict also shows that he understands weakness and urges that the monks will quietly encourage each other when it is difficult to respond readily to the call to prayer (22.5-7).

The beds of the monks consist of a mat, a woolen blanket and a light covering as well as a pillow (55.15), and a warning is given that they are not to be used to store private possessions (55.16). In a much more positive vein, however, the beds are also a place where after Sext and the meal the monks may rest in complete silence (48.5). This prescription is in the chapter that speaks of the pattern and balance of the day, so it is surely a statement about the quiet and leisure of a place—leisure in the true sense—and silence.

Outside the Gates

We do not find very much in the Rule that speaks of the monks moving outside the gates, but chapters 50 and 51 speak of what is to be done when this happens. The text shows that, in fact, the monks did move outside the gates at times. Chapter 50 discusses what is to happen when monks are working outside and cannot return to the oratory at the proper time for the Work of God. They are then to celebrate it wherever they are (50.3). Likewise, if they are sent on a journey, they are not to neglect this service. On the other hand, if the journey is short and they can return within the day, they are to refrain from eating outside (51.1). It is to this world outside the gates that some monks will return if they give in to the temptation to leave the monastery. In this case the stripping off of the monastery's clothing from the monk happens as a sign that he no longer belongs to the community (58.28). The document of profession, however, is kept and will always remain as a testimony that he once dwelt within the gates.

On the other hand, as has already been noted, there is much contact with those who dwell "outside the gates" through the guests who arrive and are welcomed (53), through those who come to the door and are greeted by the porter (66), as well as through visiting priests and monks (60 and 61). Although the Rule urges that all necessities are to be contained within the monastery and that it is better for monks not to roam outside, since this is not good for them (66.6-7), Benedict knows that the world beyond the monastery cannot be ignored.

Beyond the Gates

The Rule makes clear that Benedict knows there is another world beyond the one in which the monks are living here and now. From the Prologue to the Rule and throughout, it is clear that a journey toward something beyond this life is being undertaken. "Who yearns for life?" Benedict asks in the words of the psalm (Prol. 15; Ps 34:13). Those who respond to this call then set out on the way, clothed with faith and the performance of good works, guided by the Gospel in the search for the One who has called (Prol. 21). The Rule is in fact a description of how we are to live as we make this journey. We will always yearn for everlasting life with holy desire (4.46). We are impelled by love as we pursue everlasting life (5.10). If we fear and reverence and remember God, we will have everlasting life awaiting us (7.11). It is good zeal that leads to God and everlasting life (72.2), and the prayer at the end of this chapter is that we will be brought all together to everlasting life (72.12).

Thus, as we live our lives in this house of God, the familiar words of the psalm already quoted will be fulfilled both now and at the end of time: "One thing I asked of the LORD, that

I will seek after: to live in the house of the LORD all the days of my life, to behold the beauty of the LORD, and to inquire in his temple" (Ps 27:4).

In Jacob's dream, in which he saw the ladder set up on this earth and the top of it reaching to heaven, the Lord was standing beside him.

> The LORD . . . said, I am the LORD, the God of Abraham your father and the God of Isaac; the land on which you lie I will give to you and to your offspring; and your off-spring shall be like the dust of the earth, and you shall spread abroad to the west and to the east and to the north and to the south; and all the families of the earth shall be blessed in you and in your offspring. Know that I am with you and will keep you wherever you go and will bring you back to this land; for I will not leave you until I have done what I have promised you. (Gen 28:13-15)

No wonder that Jacob knew that this was nothing other than the "house of God" and the "gate of heaven." So too is this place, this house of God where we live the Benedictine way of life.

We are, then, nourished by the hope that the house of God, where we live out our commitment in community, will be everything Benedict expressed in his Rule. In his book *Beauty: The Invisible Embrace*, John O'Donohue speaks of how special the house of God is in all religious traditions—whether church, temple, or mosque—all places where a community gathers to hear the Word of God. His words could equally apply to how Benedict sees our own monastic dwelling places:

> When one enters there one does not simply enter a building; rather one enters unknowingly the gathered memory. This house is a living archive of transcendence. . . . The house of God is a frontier region and intense threshold where the visible world meets the ultimate but subtle structures of the invisible world. Within this sacred

space, time loses its linearity, its loneliness. It opens up and suggests itself as an ancient circle of belonging in which past and future, time lived and time to be lived, form ultimate presence. From ancient times people have understood the house of God to be the sacred ground from where it is wise to begin a journey: initiation as the journey of life in Spirit, and requiem as the beginning of the invisible journey.[8]

---

[8] John O'Donohue, *Beauty: The Invisible Embrace* (New York: Harper Collins, 2004), 160–61.

2

Benedictine Life

A Sacramental Life

AN UNDERSTANDING OF THE WORLD OF symbols is a way of deepening our experience of life. This understanding may come through literature, art, or music. It is also important in a study of the sacraments. In the area of sacramental theology the use of symbols is a key to a deeper understanding of the centrality of the seven sacraments in the life of the Church. But it also leads to a much broader area, an understanding of what I call "sacramentality" in all of life. This is the power of so much of our experience and life to reveal something beyond what is immediately apparent—something more. It can help us in our reading and study of the Rule of Benedict. Benedict may not have been explicitly thinking of sacraments or symbols or poetry when he wrote the Rule, but his use of Scripture often adds this dimension to his writing, and some of his chapters, such as the chapters on exclusion from the community, may also have been influenced by the sacramental practice of the time.

Augustine defined sacrament as "a visible form of invisible grace." In the earlier periods of Church history there was no limit of seven attached to sacraments. In fact, it was not until the Middle Ages that this notion of seven gradually became established. A defining statement that there are only seven sacraments was then made at the Council of Trent. So even in the early Church, a broader view of sacraments as a visible form of invisible grace prevailed. During the theological and liturgical renewal prior to and following Vatican II in the twentieth century, there was a rediscovery of the real fullness of the sacramental life of the Church.

We do indeed believe that the sacraments are ways by which grace is mediated, that they are a means of God's self-communication to the world. We could say with Richard McBrien that the sacraments are real, personal, and concrete symbols of God's life, the life given to humanity by God[1] and accepted and responded to gratefully by us. Ultimately, Christ himself is the sacrament of God for us, as Saint John wrote: "Something which has existed since the beginning, which we have heard, which we have seen with our own eyes, which we have watched and touched with our own hands, the Word of life—this is our theme" (1 John 1:1).

So in Christ, above all, God's life was made visible to us. We need, however, to affirm that all reality is, both potentially and in fact, a bearer of God's presence and an instrument of divine action on our behalf. A sacramental perspective is one that "sees" the divine in the human and so sees another dimension to all facets of our lives. We know that God is totally other, but we also know that God can be revealed in all things—events, people, communities, objects. Indeed, for the most part, it is only in and through these material realities that we do encounter the invisible God. "The world is charged with the grandeur of God," as Gerard Manley Hopkins says.[2] In the widest sense, again according to McBrien, the word "sacrament" applies to any finite reality through which the divine is revealed and through which our human response is shaped.[3] Everything that God has made can reveal and make

---

[1] Richard McBrien, *Catholicism* (San Francisco: Harper Collins, 1994), 9.

[2] Gerard Manley Hopkins, "God's Grandeur."

[3] McBrien, 787.

present the saving love of God. It is not surprising that we use ordinary material things as symbols in the official sacraments—bread, water, wine, oil, touch.

A symbol contains many layers of meaning. It can disclose and manifest a deeper meaning, revealing what is hidden. It can allow us to see beneath the surface, beyond the horizon, and it reaches beyond the merely rational. In the seven official sacraments of the Church these material things and gestures that I have mentioned—bread, wine, water, oil, touch—help us to penetrate the meaning of the transformative dimension of the celebration, when we really reflect on what they symbolize. So, too, do the ordinary things and events of life reveal God to us, outside the official Church celebrations. The word *mysterion*—from which we have the English word "mystery"—is the Greek equivalent of our word "sacrament," and it is the way the hidden meaning of things can be gradually revealed, the way the layers of meaning are peeled off, until we reach an inner core and see to the heart of things.

The key to reaching this inner meaning, to becoming alert to the "more" of things in the midst of the ordinary, is what some people call "awareness," or what Benedict calls "mindfulness." It is a reflectiveness about life that does not just experience things on the surface. It is being ready for the moment when we experience a sudden insight that lights up our day, or when we have to catch our breath as we experience the beauty of a work of art, or a piece of music, or a spectacular scene. In such moments we know that there is more to life than meets the eye, and we can do nothing other than praise God for this.

This mindfulness comes from living a prayerful, contemplative life where we try to live at depth. It is a result of listening which characterizes the spirituality of the whole Rule. Sister Aquinata Böckmann, a scholar on the Rule, comments that Benedict wants to lead his followers "to an integral attitude of listening, be it to God and the divine Word, be it to persons and the situation of the times, be it to the written word or the spoken word, even to the unarticulated, not yet formulated word."[4] In other words, we are to be ready to listen to God in whatever way God is revealed.

Sacrament and the Benedictine Life

So what has this to do with living the Benedictine way of life? Can this way of life be "sacramental" for us? Can it reveal God's presence in the midst of our every day and lead us to something beyond the ordinary? I would like to speak of this way of life as a revelation of God by looking at the Rule under these aspects—the people, the place, the things, and the total way of life that is thus lived. I think there is even more to say than what I am able to say at this time, but the aspects I have chosen to discuss will show that our way of life is truly sacramental. The texts will be familiar, but perhaps we can look at them in a new way.

People

> *By a bow of the head or by a complete prostration of the body, Christ is to be adored because he is indeed welcomed in them.* (53.6)

The key text I have chosen is the most obvious one and probably Benedict's clearest statement of what I am calling a sacramental perspective. In chapter 53, when speaking of the reception of guests, Benedict writes: "By a bow of the head or by a complete prostration of the body, Christ is to be adored because he is indeed welcomed in them" (53.6). On consideration, this is truly an amazing statement. It is Christ himself we are to see in the guests, quite literally. We give the guests strong marks of hospitality for this very reason. We ensure that they have a welcome, are blessed, and have suitable food and

---

[4] Aquinata Böckmann, *Perspectives on the Rule of St. Benedict* (Collegeville, MN: Liturgical Press, 1985), 16.

bedding. The chapter has opened by setting the scene with these words: "All guests who present themselves are to be welcomed as Christ, for he himself will say: 'I was a stranger and you welcomed me'" (Matt 25:35). The guest is indeed a sacrament, a revelation of Christ for us. We also reveal Christ to the guest by the ritual action of washing his feet: "The abbot with the entire community shall wash their feet" (53.14). This symbolizes our desire to serve in love. There is a very explicit statement immediately after this text in which Benedict goes on to say: "After the washing of the feet they will recite this verse: 'God, we have received your mercy in the midst of your temple'" (Ps 48:10). Surely Benedict means that both the community and the guests have received a sign of God through this welcome and its various actions and rituals.

Similarly, Benedict is clear that the abbot reveals Christ within the community: "He is believed to hold the place of Christ in the monastery, since he is addressed by a title of Christ" (2.2). This text means that the title "Abba" (father) is given to Christ, and that the abbot is to make Christ present in the monastery. He does this by his actions as he shepherds and teaches the community, as he deals compassionately with members of the community (both the weak and the strong), and as he values each one. Thus he will listen as each one gives an opinion, he will temper his behavior according to what will help individuals, and mercy and love will always be evident in his actions (see chaps. 2, 3, 27, and 64). In these ways, the abbot reflects the compassionate and loving Christ.

But it is not only the abbot who is to be an icon or sacrament of Christ in the community. The cellarer, who cares for the material goods of the monastery, is to be "like a father to the whole community." Even when unreasonable demands are made of him, he is not to reject the demanding monk but give his denial reasonably and humbly. Like Christ he is to show every care and concern for the sick, children, guests, and the poor (31.2, 7, 9). Those who care for the sick are to see Christ in those they serve, "for he said: I was sick and you visited me" (Matt 25:36) and, "What you did for one of these least brothers you did for me" (Matt 25:40; RB 36.1-3). They are to be treated with every care; but the sick, in whom we are to see Christ, are themselves to reflect Christ by their behavior so that they do not distress those who serve them.

Even serving one another in the kitchen is to be done in such a way that Christ is revealed. Those who serve are to do so in love, and they make this very real by the ritual of the washing of the feet: "Both the one who is ending his service and the one who is about to begin are to wash the feet of everyone" (35.9). This act of service is very obviously a reflection of Christ who washed the disciples' feet at the Last Supper. It is carrying out the Lord's command, "If I your Lord and Master have washed your feet, you also ought to wash one another's feet" (John 13:14).

The last individual I will mention is the porter, one who is always there when someone comes to the monastery, one who provides an answer with the warmth of love, a love that Christ showed to all who came to him.

Throughout the Rule, the behavior that is asked of all members of the community is a way of acting that will reflect Gospel values. The loving, selfless attitudes described in chapter 72, the love and mutual respect of older and younger members in chapter 71, the Gospel values of chapter 4—all of this, if lived, will enable all of us to show Christ to one another, to find Christ in one another, to be a sign and sacrament of what he taught and lived.

Place

> *The house of God should be in the care of wise men who will manage it wisely.* (53.21)

Three times in the Rule, Benedict uses the term "house of God" when speaking of the monastery. How can each house, each monastery where we live, be God's house? The term shows that whatever kind of house we live in is to be more than just a place wherein we dwell. It is to be a house of God. It is to be a house where there is a worthy steward elected to be in charge (64.5). It is to be a house which the wise will manage wisely, as the above text says (53.1). It is to be a house where there is an ordered existence as described in the chapter on the cellarer, an order that will ensure "that no one may be disquieted or distressed in the house of God" (31.19). It is to be a house where those who dwell there strive to seek God truly (58.7), where the community serves under a rule and an abbot (1.2), where God's will is the dominant factor (3.8; 5.2), where all is shared in common (33.1).

Central places in this house of God are highly symbolic and, indeed, sacramental. The oratory is one of these, and it is there that the monk expresses his desire to seek God in prayer at the Work of God: "The oratory ought to be what it is called, and nothing else is to be done or stored there" (52.1). This place becomes a symbol of our being united with God through our prayer. The fact that Benedict dedicates thirteen chapters to describing this prayer and attaches so many rituals to how it is done signifies the importance that he gives to this place (8–20). It also becomes the place where the erring brother finally is reconciled with the community through a series of rituals that show he is being gradually reintegrated into it. He comes back first to the entrance of the oratory, then he lies at the feet of all as they leave the oratory; he prostrates himself at the abbot's feet and then at the feet of all; and at last he comes to a place in the choir, though at first he cannot lead a psalm or a reading (chap. 44). The seasons themselves—summer and winter, and liturgical seasons such as Eastertide—play a large part in the organization of the monk's daily prayer.

Another "sacramental" place in the house of God is the table. Once more Benedict pays great attention to this place which holds a central place in the community. Like the oratory, it is the place from which the erring monk is excluded, thus representing his exclusion from the community. Three chapters (39–41) are given to the meals of the brothers, and one to the spiritual nourishment that is given at the table by the reader (38). Chapter 35 describes in detail the way the brothers who serve in the kitchen are to operate, their care of the materials, towels and utensils, their prayer as they begin and end their week of service, and the care that is to be given to them so that they can carry out their duties well. One cannot help making connections that are eucharistic, since Benedict obviously believes that the table is such an important part of belonging to and being transformed within the community. The way the brothers are to wash the feet of all before their gift of service in love, ought to remind us of the Last Supper. Thus, these two places in the house of God are sacraments of how the community is to live. They are places of union with and belonging to God and one another.

Two other images also take us to a deeper meaning of how Benedict sees the house of God. The community, the house of God, is a school where we both practice and learn discipleship (Prol. 45), and it is a workshop where we use and live the tools of the Gospel, thus finally reaching the reward of eternal life (4.75-78).

Material Goods

He will regard all utensils and goods of the monastery as sacred vessels of the altar. (31.10)

This is another amazing text, so familiar that sometimes we fail to see its significance. Just as the house where we dwell is more than an ordinary dwelling, so too do the material things we use have another meaning. Sometimes we can feel it is surprising that Benedict can give so much attention to the ordinary things of life—food, clothing, bedding, crafts. But if what I am saying about the sacramental aspect of our life is true, it is not so surprising. One text I always think shows

Benedict's attitude in this connection is found in chapter 35.
When he is speaking of the brother who is completing his
week of service doing the washing, he mentions the towels
in verse 8, then everyone's feet in verse 9, and the utensils in
verse 10. You notice that he does not put the feet of the people
first. I suspect that for Benedict the care of the utensils and
the towels also assumes great importance. As the opening
text suggests, everything is sacred, nothing is profane, and
our attitude to and use of everything can be a revelation of
God to us.

In chapter 32, "On the Tools and Goods of the Monastery,"
this attitude is evident. One in whom the abbot has confidence
is to be in charge of the goods, and all are to treat these with
reverence and respect, being accountable for keeping them
clean and returning them after use. Two more chapters on
material things follow, and how we view these becomes a test
of our desire to give up everything. There is to be no private
ownership; and why not? Because "monks may not have the
free disposal even of their own bodies and wills" (33.4). If we
want to possess material things, this is a sign that the gift of
self is not being lived fully. Our acceptance of the way goods
are to be distributed according to need, makes them a sign of
our willingness to live in harmony with others, without envy
or murmuring. Again, goods are more than mere things.

There is more in chapters 39 and 40 than just a description
of the food and drink that monks may have. These chapters
counsel consideration for those with individual weaknesses
by prescribing for them two dishes, and even a third, when
fresh fruit or vegetables are available. There is not just a pound
of bread provided, but a generous pound. Something additional is provided when the work is heavy. Though there is
balance here in the prescriptions, and frugality is a key virtue,
the text does indeed show something of the generosity of a
loving God. To make sure that we do not miss this point,
chapter 41, "On the Times for the Brothers' Meals," reminds
us that the "abbot should so regulate and arrange all matters

that souls may be saved and the brothers may go about their activities without justifiable grumbling" (41.5).

There is much that could be said about what clothing is provided, but I would make the point again that there is a care for individuals exhibited by the fact that the abbot is to be concerned that the garments are fitted to the wearer (55.8). In the same way as for other goods, care for clothing is described, and even worn clothing is to be returned when new articles are received. We cannot miss the symbolic significance of clothing in Benedict's eyes, in the stripping of the monk's own clothing and his clothing in what belongs to the monastery, in the chapter "On the Reception of Brothers." The ordinance is very powerful: "Then and there in the oratory, he is to be stripped of everything of his own that he is wearing and clothed in what belongs to the monastery" (58.26). This is further emphasized in the fact that, if that brother ever chooses to leave the monastery, he is to be stripped of the clothing of the monastery at that point (58.28). Here, the clothing becomes a symbol of belonging, and there is a further symbol used here, too. The document the monk has signed during the ceremony where he expresses what he is promising had been laid on the altar. But if the monk leaves, though the clothing of his former life is returned to him, that document remains forever in the monastery, signifying that he has once belonged to the community (58.19, 29).

All Together to Everlasting Life

Clothed, then, with faith and the performance of good works, let us set out on this way with the Gospel for our guide, that we may deserve to see him who has called us to his kingdom. (Prol. 21)

An important aspect of sacraments and symbols is that there always remains more that can be revealed about the meaning of things. This is very evident in the Rule when Benedict speaks about the way of life of the community. The way of life is to be treasured in itself, everything in it is to be valued, but we are often reminded that this life leads to a life beyond and is even a reflection of it now. He frequently refers to "eternal life." Our yearning for life when the Lord calls us is more than a yearning for life in this world. What we do now is leading us to eternal life. We will dwell in the tent of the kingdom if we run there by doing good deeds (Prol. 22). Even more clearly, "If we wish to reach eternal life, even as we avoid the torments of hell, then while there is still time, while we are in the body and have time to accomplish all these things by the light of life—we must run and do now what will profit us forever" (Prol. 42-43). Our patient sharing in the sufferings of Christ will make us deserve also to share in his kingdom (Prol. 50). It is love that impels us to pursue everlasting life and makes us eager to take the narrow road, because this road leads to life (5.10-11).

The great image of the ladder of humility makes the connection of this life and the next very explicit. The ladder is grounded in our life in this world and, through the wholeness of our persons (our body and soul are the sides of this ladder, he says), we are led to heaven. This speaks to me of transformation of our earthly life into eternal life. Now the ladder erected is our life on earth and, if we humble our hearts, the Lord will raise it to heaven (RB 7.8). Toward the end of the Rule, Benedict poses the question, "Are you hastening toward your heavenly home?" and he goes on, "Then with Christ's help, keep this little rule we have written for beginners" (73.8). So he has no doubt that this way of life, which is set out in the Rule, is a way to the fullness of eternal life.

It is no wonder Benedict says that we are to yearn for everlasting life with holy desire (4.77). This longing for eternal life is constant in people of faith. Remember that Saint John has said, "God gave us eternal life, and this life is in his Son. Whoever has the Son has life" (1 John 5:11-12); and he also says, "I write these things to you who believe in the name of the Son of God, so that you may know that you have eternal life" (1 John 5:13).

This longing is often expressed beautifully in the tradition, for example when Ignatius of Antioch says: "How good it is to be sinking down below the world's horizon toward God, to rise again later into the dawn of his presence."[5] What we are doing is what Teilhard de Chardin describes as giving "of one's deepest to that whose depth has no end."[6] Saint Augustine says that, in our time of pilgrimage, we see the vision of eternal life only through "an enigmatic parable"; but we must "bend our ear to this parable," listen to its meaning.[7] Saint Ambrose also says it clearly: "Do not believe your natural sight only. What is not seen is more truly seen, for this is eternal, while the other is temporal. We see more truly what is not perceptible to the eyes but is discerned by the mind and the soul."[8]

If we can see the deeper meaning of our lives in this world, in whatever way of life we have chosen to live, if we can find God in the events, things, places, and people of our lives, then we will one day see something beyond all of this, and we will understand the whole of the meaning of our present life. Benedict ends chapter 4, "On the Tools for Good Works," with these great words: "These then, are the tools of the spiritual craft. When we have used them without ceasing day and night and have returned them on judgment day, our wages will be

[5] Ignatius of Antioch, "Epistle to the Romans," 2, in *Early Christian Writings: The Apostolic Fathers*, trans. Maxwell Staniforth (Middlesex: Penguin Books, 1968), 104.

[6] Pierre Teilhard de Chardin, *The Divine Milieu: An Essay on the Interior Life* (London: Collins, 1961), 118.

[7] Augustine, *Exposition on the Psalms*, trans. Maria Boulding (Hyde Park, NY: New City Press, 1990), 356.

[8] P. Schaff and H. Wace, eds., *Select Library of Nicene and Post-Nicene Fathers of the Christian Church* (Grand Rapids, MI: Eerdmans, 1989), 318.

the reward the Lord has promised. 'What the eye has not seen nor the ear heard, God has prepared for those who love him' (1 Cor 2:9)." And where do we use these tools? In our life in this world: "The workshop where we are to toil faithfully at all these tasks is the enclosure of the monastery and stability in the community" (4.75-78). I think Benedict would agree with Australian author David Malouf when he speaks of his imaginary Ister River in his book *An Imaginary Life:*

> It has been there always, somehow waiting, even as my eye noted it on maps, as the final boundary of my life, waiting to be crossed, and patient year after year for my arrival. However many steps I may have taken away from it, both in reality and in my mind, it remained, shifting its tides, freezing each season, cracking up, flowing again, whispering to me: *I am the border beyond which you must go if you are to find your true life, your true death at last.*[9]

Our life and all that is part of it is, indeed, a revelation of God. We have to go beyond the border of this present life to find a deeper meaning. Then our lives are truly sacramental.

[9] David Malouf, *An Imaginary Life* (London: Chatto and Windus, 1978), 136.

3

An Adventure Tale of Divine Love

ASCETICISM MAY NOT IMMEDIATELY bring to mind the thought of adventure tales and divine love. Most people's views of asceticism, influenced by stories of rigorous and austere practices, especially amongst those who sought solitude in the desert, would probably not evoke thoughts of adventure and love. Asceticism can often signify, not freedom, but submission to irksome rules; not beauty, but harsh rigor; not joy, but gloomy austerity. Can we believe that asceticism produces not only a good but also, indeed, a *beautiful* personality? Often the early Christian themes of sexual renunciation, bodily fasting, and solitude carry for us icy overtones.[1] Peter Brown, a well-known writer in the area, claims that it is up to modern scholarship to bring to these practices their due measure of warmth and to restore to them a little of the weight they once carried.[2]

---

[1] Kallistos Ware, "The Way of the Ascetics: Negative or Affirmative?" in *Asceticism*, ed. V. Wimbush and R. Valantasis (New York: Oxford University Press, 1995), 3–4.

[2] Peter Brown, *The Body and Society: Men, Women, and Sexual Renunciation in Early Christianity* (New York: Columbia University Press, 1988), 446–47.

There are many questions about asceticism that could be addressed, questions such as the central place ascetical practices hold in the worldview and lifestyle of those who live the Christian and monastic life. But in this chapter I will limit myself to examining the understanding of asceticism in early monasticism, and more importantly, how it affects our present day living of the monastic life.

In order to approach both of these aspects, it is necessary to examine two points that underlie a balanced understanding of asceticism: (1) the connection between asceticism and the body, and (2) the need to develop a positive view of asceticism.

The Body

It could be said that asceticism is central to everything human and Christian because, in fact, it concerns the centrality of the body and is about the transformation or transfiguration of our bodies into the resurrected Body of Christ. We bring our whole selves, including our bodies, in commitment to Christ, just as in the Eucharist we hear his own words, "This is my body given for you." We pledge our body to the place where, and the people with whom, we live our lives. We are here reminded of the monk who asked for help and received the reply, "Give your body in pledge to the walls of your cell."[3] In our bodies, always located in this particular place, is where we discover who we are and how we are to be holy; the same cannot occur in some fantasy world where we think all would be well only because, in fact, we would be seeking a world we could control.

This body, so grippingly present to us, is the body that God has afforded us as a field to cultivate where we might work and become rich.[4] This is what the incarnation is about. God

---

[3] Rowan Williams, *Silence and Honey Cakes: The Wisdom of the Desert* (Oxford: Lion Books, 2004), 89.

[4] Brown, 236.

anchored divine life in a body. Christ was made human. Such an attitude gives us a *whole* view of things, and it also gives us hope that, with Gregory the Great, we could ask for the grace to see life whole and the power to speak effectively of it.[5]

Benedict

Benedict uses the idea of the body *(corpus)* in relation to asceticism. In the chapter "On the Tools for Good Works" (4.11-13), following the phrase, "To deny one's own self in order to follow Christ" (4.10), is the text "To chastise the body" (4.11). This is then followed by other "bodily" aspects, although the word *corpus* is not used: "not to embrace delicacies, to love · fasting, and to give new life to the poor" (4.12-14). Surely this is a true understanding of fasting, the idea that I fast so that I might have something to give to others.

The other important occasion when the idea of body is used comes in chapter 49, "On Lent." We are urged in Lent to withdraw from the body, food, drink, sleep, talk, jesting. Here we have a list of ascetical practices (49.7).

In the chapter on the abbot, Benedict says there is to be a chastising of the body if the person is evil or stubborn, arrogant or disobedient (2.28). This indicates the expectation that the chastising of the body will change our dispositions.

Sometimes Benedict's tool for good works titled "To deny oneself [one's body] in order to follow Christ" (4.10), and the impact of the gospel passage it is drawn from (Matt 16:24; Luke 9:23), can be lost on us. But we must ask who this Christ is whom we are following and into whom we are being transformed. It is not the historical figure, but the transfigured, crucified, risen, ascended Christ, the Christ of the Eucharist, the Christ we meet in the body of Christ, the Church, and

---

[5] From a homily on the book of Ezekiel in *The Liturgy of the Hours according to the Roman Rite*, v. 3 (London: Collins, 1975), 233.

in each other in the community, a community consisting of persons, of bodies. There are no abstract members. And, of course, to follow is not just to walk behind or even to imitate. It is a process of incorporation, being made one-body-with, being transformed so that we are indeed found *in Christ*. If denying oneself is the way to this, then we can claim it is well worth doing. The cost for everyone may be the same, namely, death; but we must indeed die in order to enter the realm of the kingdom, in order *to be Christ*. This surely is the goal of all our ascetical efforts.

Not a Negative Concept

Asceticism does not have to do simply with the negative and it does not have to do with the distant past. Kallistos Ware argues that the cultural construction of asceticism as purely negative lacks nuance. Both for those who practiced it in the past and for those who practice it now, the positive and life-giving aspects must be discovered and articulated. He says that moderation is the key, and what basically distinguishes natural from un-natural asceticism is its attitude toward the body.[6] The goal is not at all maiming the body, tormenting it, inflicting pain on it. All that this would show would be a hatred for God's creation.

There is, however, a basic tension in the early literature between the hagiographical genre, with often extreme ac-counts, and other genres that urge moderation. Sometimes these tensions are found even within the same text. Attitudes are often ambivalent and language is ambiguous.[7] Perhaps the tension and struggle is always there. Even at the heights of mysticism, there is still the need for bodily discipline, vigils, fasting, solitude, self-control. But the categories cannot dis-

---

[6] Ware, "The Way of the Ascetics," 9.

[7] Gail Corrington-Streete, "Trajectories of Ascetic Behavior: Re-sponse to the Three Preceding Papers," in Wimbush and Valantasis, 121.

guise the fact that it is one and the same person who is the ascetic and the mystic.[8]

Basically, we must believe that we practice asceticism not because we think the world ugly but to remove any obstacle that will prevent us seeing that the world is an anticipatory reflection of the kingdom—a sacrament—and that in this world we already experience and encounter the presence and reign of God. Those who went into the desert did so to carry out a radical experiment in disciplined life. They wanted to see what it took to order a life to God.

Another point here is that ascetical renunciation does not imply that what is renounced is bad. Rather, what happens is that, by a free choice and decision, a lower (or at least different) good is given up for the sake of a higher good. For example, we renounce unlimited freedom of movement, by stability; marriage, by celibacy; autonomy, by obedience; but all the things that are here renounced are good in themselves.

Therefore, basic to all discussions on asceticism are these two points: first, that it is about the body; and, second, that there is need to stress a very positive view of asceticism.

If one considers ascetical practices as methods and programs designed to restrain the influence of sin and to maximize union with God, most aspects of Benedict's way of life could be considered "ascetical." For example, the chapter on Lent begins, "At all times the lifestyle of a monk ought to have a Lenten quality" (49.1). Terence Kardong calls this chapter a gentle and serene approach to monastic life.[9] It covers so many aspects of our cenobitic life—silence, prayer, reading, desire, the interactions among individuals, community, and abbot—all of which are ascetical practices. One could also

---

[8] Teresa M. Shaw, "Practical, Theoretical, and Cultural Tracings in Late Ancient Asceticism: Response to the Three Preceding Papers," in Wimbush and Valantasis, 76.

[9] Terrence Kardong, *Benedict's Rule: A Translation and Commentary* (Collegeville, MN: Liturgical Press, 1996), 408.

consider discussing asceticism within the framework of two key elements of our ascetical endeavor, namely, humility and obedience (together with authority).

What Is Asceticism?

The word "asceticism," derived from the Greek *askesis,* indicates athletic training, exercise, practice or discipline, and there are many ways of interpreting it. Teresa Shaw claims that, in antiquity, *askesis* could apply to any regimen of exercise with a goal of improvement—in performance, in manner of life, or in health and effectiveness of body and mind. Borrowing from athletic terminology, it became a metaphor implying rigorous dedication, hard work, and discipline to the point of self-denial in a particular philosophical or religious mode of life.

Shaw makes the point that ascetic disciplines may involve bodily renunciations (for example, sexual chastity, abstinence from food, poverty, or contemplative disciplines such as meditation or study). She understands asceticism as a way of life that requires daily discipline and is intentionality applied to bodily behaviors. It is a positive valuation of training and self-management for a particular goal or way of life. This can be an individual option, but rigorous observance of such behaviors can also define a particular group and be a factor in determining group status.[10]

Another way of looking at asceticism is to note that, just like any other serious pursuit, monastic life has its own skills and training regimens, and it is these various disciplines of the monastic way that we put under the heading of "asceticism." So the word implies any practices that "train" us to live our way of life.[11]

---

[10] Teresa M. Shaw, *The Burden of the Flesh: Fasting and Sexuality in Early Christianity* (Minneapolis, MN: Fortress Press, 1998), 29.

[11] C. Stewart, *Prayer and Community: The Benedictine Tradition* (London: Darton, Longman and Todd, 1998), 89.

Asceticism is thus an aspect of the liberation of the human person, and is "a concentration of inner forces and command of oneself."[12] The process relates to our human dignity and leads to self-mastery and the fulfilment of our goals.

A modern scholar on desert spirituality, Rowan Williams, the former archbishop of Canterbury, says that asceticism is simply about the purification of seeing, a way of opening our eyes to our true self before God, about learning to contain that aspect of human acquisitiveness that leads us to compete.[13]

Asceticism and Monasticism

Monasticism inherited an earlier tradition of ascetic theology and practice. In the end, it became the cornerstone for it and the place where it could develop. It was also a place where its fruits could be handed down through spiritual teaching.[14]

Monasticism was able to develop Christian teaching from the Gnostic tradition, incorporating certain mystical ideas, in particular taking over from later Greek philosophy the idea of *theoria*. This idea was then used to describe not just any philosophical observation, as previously, but also the contemplative vision of the divine. The companion idea of *praktiké* now came to signify the active love of neighbor, as in the *agape* enjoined in the New Testament, and not just in the public life of the citizen of the polis.[15] The important thing here is not to dichotomize the spiritual life as consisting of *theoria* over against *praktiké* as its contrary concept.

---

[12] Ware, "The Way of the Ascetics," 3.

[13] ABC Radio Broadcast, May 2001.

[14] Samuel Rubenson, "Christian Asceticism and the Emergence of the Monastic Tradition," in Wimbush and Valantasis, 49.

[15] Bernard McGinn, "Asceticism and Mysticism in Late Antiquity and the Early Middle Ages," in Wimbush and Valantasis, 61.

Louis Bouyer calls the asceticism of monastic life "the first complete system of Christian spirituality."[16] In other words, monastic asceticism addresses the whole person and how the person stands before God.

Life a Whole and Not an Either/Or

The concept of the wholeness of life may be found in so many early Christian texts that speak of our monastic disciplines and practices. There are many examples in the Rule where Benedict expresses this wholeness of outlook. Often conjunctions such as "and," "but," and "in order to" are either stated or implied in his text when Benedict is attempting to make various linkages and connections in his ideas.

Some good examples are in the Gospel teaching of chapter 4. Here we read: "To deny oneself *in order to* follow Christ" (4.10); "To confess one's sins to God *and* change our evil ways" (4.57 and 58); "To love fasting *and* to give new life to the poor" (4.13 and 14); "To keep custody at every hour over the actions of one's life *and* to know with certainty that God sees one in every place" (4.48 and 49); "To respect the elders *and* to love the young" (4.70 and 71). Seeming opposites are linked by Benedict: "To attribute whatever good one sees in oneself to God, not to oneself, *but* always to clearly acknowledge and take personal responsibility for the evil one does" (42 and 43); "To fear the day of judgment, to dread Hell, *and* to desire eternal life with all ardent longing" (4.44, 45, 46). The list could go on and on. It is very liberating to read the Rule in this way, noting connections and becoming immersed in Benedict's holistic view of life.

It is clear that certainly in the ascetic practices of the ancients there was no idea of theory versus practice, or contemplation

[16] Louis Bouyer, *The Spirituality of the New Testament and the Fathers* (New York: Seabury, 1982), 381, as quoted in McGinn, "Asceticism and Mysticism in Late Antiquity," 65.

versus *askesis,* or spiritual versus physical, or work versus prayer, or even of the body/soul dichotomy that was apparently such a strong Greek influence. It is interesting to ask ourselves how it came to be that these dichotomies, in the end, held such power in Christian lives and, in fact, perhaps still do. Can we shift to language and constructions expressive of the practices and relationships of the fully human person? In this view, asceticism has a unitive function. David Fagerberg uses a wonderful image about the liturgy which I think we could apply to this concept of asceticism: "Like a needle pulling thread through fabric to stitch up a rent cloth, [a holistic asceticism] moves in and out, in and out, between earth and heaven, eternity and time, the sacred and the profane, plunging into one and then the other and drawing them together by the thread of [our lives]."[17]

Asceticism is really a statement about the relationship between the body, the soul, and the human potential for salvation.[18] Yet the irony is that, though we may grasp this holistic attitude, put aside in theory body/soul splits, and value the body, yet we still drink and eat too much, we are still driven by ambition, we are sad and worried, we lack discipline, knowing that all of this affects a balanced and holistic view of life.

The great Byzantine theologian Symeon places his ascetical teaching in the context of the Beatitudes, the basic manifesto of the Christian life. As in Benedict, so here in the Gospel we find a most positive view of holiness: "Blessed are the poor in spirit, *for* theirs is the kingdom." Symeon begins his teaching on the spiritual life with the strongest possible ascetical statement: "Whoever desires to find God, let him deny himself."

---

[17] David W. Fagerberg, "A Century of Consequences," in *Theologia Prima: What Is Liturgical Theology?*, 2nd ed. (Chicago: Hillenbrand Books, 2004), 228.

[18] Susanna Elm, *"Virgins of God": The Making of Asceticism in Late Antiquity* (Oxford: Clarendon Press, 1996), 373.

For Symeon, the Beatitudes represent a wholeness of ascetical behavior and mystical perception.[19]

It is an interesting exercise to look at the practices behind the Beatitudes, as well as noting their very positive view. For example, if we say "Blessed are the poor in spirit *for* theirs is the kingdom of heaven," we note that self-emptying and dependence on God are the characteristics that form the background to poverty of spirit. Gentleness, mercy, and peace-making presuppose a particular attitude and practice in our relationships. This same thing could be traced through all the teaching of the Beatitudes.

In the article already cited, Kallistos Ware sums up much of this question. He speaks of asceticism as the liberation of the human person, as the concentration of inner forces and as command of oneself. This is related to our human dignity. It leads to self-mastery and enables us to fulfill the purpose that we have set for ourselves. We all know that such ascetical discipline is a necessary aspect of all that we undertake, whether scholarship, politics, athletics, prayer, or wholesome daily living. "Without this ascetic concentration of effort," Ware writes, "we are at the mercy of exterior forces or our own emotions or moods; we lack inner freedom. Sometimes we have to have an attitude that does not ignore the immediate, but denies the immediate the right to prevail. Only the ascetic is inwardly free."[20]

In the tradition, two basic components of the ascetical life are often emphasized: *anachoresis* ("withdrawal from the world") and *enkrateia* ("self-control").[21]

---

[19] *Symeon the New Theologian: The Discourses*, trans. C. J. De Catanzaro (Mahwah, NJ: Paulist Press, 1980), 47.

[20] Ware, "The Way of the Ascetics," 3.

[21] In Basil of Caesarea, for example, these ideas are very strong. See Augustine Holmes, *A Life Pleasing to God: The Spirituality of the Rules of St Basil* (London: Darton, Longman, and Todd, 2000), 107–10 ("Longer Rule 5"), 241–43 ("Longer Rule 19").

Withdrawal

The question is, how can one make these aspects of asceticism world-affirming rather than world-denying? There is the example of people like Antony and Benedict, both of whom withdrew into solitude. According to Athanasius, Antony lived in solitude in a ruined fort for two decades. Finally, after many years, his friends broke down the door and he came out, looking none the worse for his rigorous life of self-control. Though he did not leave the desert, for the next fifty years he gave guidance to many and helped a multitude of disciples.[22] So, too, with Benedict. First there were his contacts with the monk in the cave, then with the shepherds, and finally his founding of various monasteries. The ascetics of the desert were looking for solitude, not isolation. In their case, silence eventually gave way to speech, and seclusion led to involvement.

Precisely because they first withdrew into solitude could such people afterward act as spiritual guides. They fled not in order to prepare themselves for any task, but to be alone with God. One thing is integral to the other. The flight was for the quest for God, free of other concerns. It was part of the human being's return to self and to God. Asceticism is not a goal in itself, but a way to open oneself to what God wants to give. Kallistos Ware observes: "Often it is precisely the men and women of inner stillness—not the activists but the contemplatives, fired by a consuming passion for solitude—who in practice bring about the most far-reaching alterations in the society around them."[23] Antony says that both our life and our death occur alongside our neighbor, so in a way we flee for the sake of community.[24]

---

[22] Athanasius, *The Life of Antony and the Letter to Marcellinus*, ed. Robert C. Gregg, The Classics of Western Spirituality (New York: Paulist Press, 1980), 87.

[23] Ware, "The Way of the Ascetics," 6.

[24] Benedicta Ward, ed., *Sayings of the Desert Fathers*, Cistercian Studies Series 59 (Kalamazoo, MI: Cistercian Publications, 1984), 9.

The desert is a place where God is to be found. It is the place where Moses saw God face to face, and it is also the place where the demons dwell. So there is a need for struggle there and for the exercise of self-control. But the purpose of fleeing to the desert is not to escape but rather to encounter. Such withdrawal, therefore, by definition, is not self-centered.[25] It is a way of opening one's eyes to areas that are obstacles to our own and others' paths to God. It is an effort to find the truth about ourselves, to come to purity of heart. This does require discipline, self-control, and asceticism, and this path is always to be undertaken solely in order to find life. It is not about ignoring human needs but rather about refusing to cater to one's own excessive desires.

What those who went to the desert were fleeing was illusion; and so we, too, seek a withdrawal like theirs in order to find the space to become who we truly are before God. We flee, in fact, for the sake of the community. We flee the chains of obsessions, fantasies, and status. We withdraw from the self-definition that comes from artificial "short-cuts" which can give us no depth. We flee self-justification and the projections of others. We are silent so as not to extinguish God's Word in us. We are silent so that we can recognize the way we slip from the truth of what we are. It is a quiet and gentle self-monitoring. We move into a stillness where God can draw us to himself.[26]

Self-Control

Asceticism is about refinement, transformation. It is a striving to reach purity of heart. Again here we have the example of Antony. It is said that he emerged from his long solitude and

---

[25] Ware, "The Way of the Ascetics," 7.

[26] Rowan Williams, talk at the 2001 John Main Seminar, Sydney, July 15–18, broadcast by the Australian Broadcasting Commission.

many trials altogether balanced, as one guided by reason and abiding in the natural state.

Susanna Elm, a specialist in early Christian virginity, says that asceticism is not about transcending the body but about transforming it. In the early Church, a rigorously disciplined body was a direct sign of divine stability and, therefore, of sanctity.[27] The body acquired a new significance from what it had in pagan antiquity. As the dramatic symbol of the sole saving force—the incarnate, embodied Son—the physical body itself becomes the locus of transformation and, thus, of salvation.

Apparently the goal envisioned here is not to mortify the passions but to redirect them; not to eradicate but to educate them; not to eliminate but to transfigure them. If this were to happen, then we arrive at the state of *apatheia*, a condition of inner freedom and integration in which we are not under the domination of sinful impulses and therefore we become capable of genuine love. Then, "nothing can separate us from the love of God" (see Rom 8:35). This is Cassian's purity of heart. Sometimes *apatheia* is called a fire, in the sense that our burning love for God and others leaves no room for sinful impulses. We see then that for the Greek Fathers, *enkrateia* (self-control), which is the practical means toward *apatheia*, means a reintegration of body and spirit and a transformation of the passions. These early fathers are advocating not repression but transfiguration.

Transformation

There has to be an eschatological dimension to this endeavor, lest our ascetical practices are to degenerate to merely physical practices comparable to training for sports, as Columba Stewart notes:

> Asceticism [can] become a set of behaviors or a form of discourse that floats free from spiritual motivations. . . .

[27] Elm, *"Virgins of God,"* 379.

But surely the fundamental conviction that a life of prayer and ascetical discipline would bring the practitioner closer to God in this world, and prepare him for the next, underlies any Christian ascetical commitment, whatever else might have been going on.[28]

But we need a correct view of eschatology, understanding it as a here-and-now reality and not only as something ahead of us and unattainable. Our practice comes out of life's circumstances and is a response of love to what life brings here and now.

The real ends of the ascetical life are not social, economic, or political, but ultimately eschatological. There are different ways of expressing this reality: as the memory of God, the life of inner prayer, the contemplative state, a mind carried beyond itself. But this inner attitude is dependent on, expressed in, and nourished by the basic ascetical practices, that is, fasting, vigils, obedience, work, service, guarding the mind, and celibacy—all of which create inner space in the heart for union with God.

Here again Symeon is an example of this. His central theme is that of the personal experience of the paschal mystery through the practice of asceticism. He shows how the resurrection passes from the historical and liturgical dimensions into that of personal spiritual experience in such a way that the ascetic participates in Christ's mysteries and makes them his or her own. He describes how the divine wisdom awakens the sleeping soul, which recognizes God as it awakes and is carried away in love toward God. Asceticism detaches the senses from the everyday world, yet without removing the monk from it, in order to allow inner sensation to blossom. Thus it is that the resurrection happens in the heart of the

[28] Columba Stewart, "'Asceticism': A Feature Review," review of *Asceticism*, ed. V. Wimbush and R. Valantasis, *The American Benedictine Review* 48, no. 3 (1997): 258.

monk. Asceticism must be driven by the sense of Christ, the memory of Christ.[29]

One accepts the material world and the material body in the belief of and hope for its transformation. The human body is destined to be transformed into an awesome model, a resplendent vehicle, a temple of God. The transformation of the microcosm—the body—will entail the experience of the transformed macrocosm, the world.

Transformation is possible because of unconditional love, since the kenotic love of Christ in us calls forth from us the same love. It is not a selfish love, but a love very much in touch with the needs of the world.

Another way of expressing this is that we must die to self so that a new self can be born. We must free ourselves for God. We must die to our old life and rise to new life. This is the meaning of the great paschal mystery (see Rom 6:1-11; Phil 2:6-11; Eph 4:23-24). A contemporary example of the experience of this mystery of death and life is offered us by a poignant press photo of women who were pregnant when their husbands died in the United States on September 11, 2001. The photo shows them with their new babies, born after the event. This is surely new life for them after the terrible experience of suffering they had endured when their husbands were killed in the terrorist attack.

Cassian's point of view is that asceticism is a therapeutic tool to recondition, under grace, the reactions of body and mind. Hence all our actions, even those we perform spontaneously without much forethought, can come into harmony with our intention to love God, our neighbor, and ourselves. The aim is that all we are or do should be rooted in God.[30]

---

[29] Gregory Collins, "Simeon the New Theologian: An Ascetical Theology for Middle-Byzantine Monks," in Wimbush and R. Valantasis, 346–47.

[30] Cassian, *Conference* 10.7.1, in Ramsey, *John Cassian: The Conferences*, 375.

Our Lives

In conclusion, we must ask what the implications of all of this might be, for our lives in the present, for the way of life we have chosen, for the solitude we seek, and for the community to which we are committed. What are the practices in our lives that lead to transformation of our whole selves into Christ? David Fagerberg writes:

> The attempt to understand asceticism will always end in failure unless one admits the possibility of wild, bracing divine love. At the end of his biography of Francis, Chesterton treats the story of Claire running away at the tender age of seventeen to become a nun, and suggests viewing it as St. Francis helping Claire to elope into the cloister, since the scene had many of the elements of a regular romantic elopement. She escaped through a hole in the wall, fled against her father's wishes, and was received at midnight by the light of torches. "Now about that incident, I will here only say this. If it had really been a romantic elopement and the girl had become a bride instead of a nun, practically the whole modern world would have made her a heroine. . . . The point for the moment is that modern romanticism entirely encourages such defiance of parents when it is done in the name of romantic love. For it knows that romantic love is a reality, but it does not know that divine love is a reality."[31]

The point of the asceticism of the desert monks, and the point of it for us now, can be expressed in the following way: "The professed ascetics are walking adventure tales of divine love who awaken our eagerness for whatever wild ascetical adventure will be required of each of us in order to go home."[32]

---

[31] David W. Fagerberg, "A Century on Liturgical Asceticism," in *On Liturgical Asceticism* (Washington, DC: The Catholic University of America Press, 2013), 226.

[32] Fagerberg, 228.

4

Authority

A Service of Love

ALL MEMBERS OF THE COMMUNITY ARE called by Benedict into a life of mutual service and obedience. We have responded willingly and eagerly to the call of God to live in obedience. The mutuality of our living is expressed in the relationships of one to another, of the abbot to the members of the community and vice versa, and of all of us to God. The Rule reveals clearly, however, that those who are called to lead the community and those who hold any position of authority in the community are called very explicitly to this service. When the text of the Rule is examined, such an attitude is expressed in the words Benedict uses, sometimes repeatedly, as well as in the Scripture texts he chooses and in the emphasis he gives to such positions in the community. It is clear that the abbot holds a special place in the community, and other members—such as the cellarer, the deans, the porter, the kitchen servers, those who welcome the guests and care for the sick—all exercise their roles in a spirit of service. The service is always a service of love.

In chapter 63, "On Rank in the Community," there is a strong reference to this call to service. Benedict says: "But the abbot, because we believe that he holds the place of Christ, is to be called 'lord' and 'abbot,' not for any claim of his own but out of honor and love for Christ. He, for his part, must reflect on this, and in his behavior show himself worthy of such honor"

(63.13-14). We can sense here a close connection with the episode and language of the description of the washing of the feet at the Last Supper: "After he had washed their feet, had put on his robe, and had returned to the table, he said to them, 'Do you know what I have done to you? You call me Teacher and Lord—and you are right for that is what I am. So if I, your Lord and Teacher, have washed your feet, you also ought to wash one another's feet. For I have set you an example, that you also should do as I have done to you'" (John 13:12-14). The titles "lord," "abbot," and "teacher" simply bring with them an obligation of service. Never is the abbot "to disturb the flock entrusted to him nor make any unjust arrangements as though he had power to do whatever he wished" (63.3). His behavior is to reflect that to which he is called, just as Christ showed by his example.

An expression of how this behavior is to manifest itself is revealed in the examination of the texts of the Rule which deal with the abbot and any other member of the community who has a special role of service. It is possible to obtain a strong sense of this by grouping words that Benedict uses in his descriptions of what is to characterize such people. They could be grouped under such headings as "love," "care," "humility," "wisdom," and "fear of the Lord." Then, within each of these contexts, we will find such people acting in a discerning way—in service, reflectively, worthily, and always aware of their own frailty.

Essential Qualities of Service

a) Love and Care

The three Latin words for love (*amor, caritas,* and *dilectio*) appear often in the section of the Rule that refers to those who hold positions of authority in the community. Love makes possible the abbot's ability to teach and the community's ability to hear and obey. It is the love between them that makes everything possible.[1] We hear that the abbot must strive to be loved rather than feared (64.15), and he is to show equal love to all (2.17, 22). Love is to be shown to those who err. The abbot is to hate the faults and love the brothers (64.11). Faults are to be pruned away with prudence and love as he sees best for the individual (64.14), and even when the monk is excluded from the community, the abbot must affirm him in love (27.4). Other officials in the monastery are also to exercise love. The porter is to respond to calls with the warmth of love (66.4), the sick are to be served by one who is loving (36.7), and the seniors are to love the juniors (63.10). There can be no doubt that love is the basis of all relationships in the monastery.

The word *cura*, meaning both "care" and "cure," appears frequently. The word *gerere* is often linked with *cura* as though the abbot had to "wage" care. The same attitude is expressed in his use of *sollicitudo* and *custodia*. Both care and cure flow from an attitude of love for one another. It is the kind of care that comes from being attentive to one another, from recognizing what the other can bear at the moment and then acting accordingly. The abbot takes very seriously his responsibility for those in his care (2.38). Benedict does not speak of the members of community as those whom the abbot governs or rules, but rather as "those in his care." Terrence Kardong notes that, as in the case of Christ, the troubled member is not a distraction to the "real" business of the abbot; the troubled member *is* the abbot's business par excellence.[2] The abbot has to exercise utmost care, great concern for all—*omni sollicitudine curam gerat* (27.1, 33, 39). Even the wayward are to experience this care (27.1, 5; 28.5), and the abbot must always strive to cure those who have strayed (2.8, 10). The health of all is to be the goal of all decision making (3.5).

[1] Columba Stewart, *Prayer and Community* (Maryknoll, NY: Orbis Books, 1998), 83.

[2] Terrence Kardong, *Benedict's Rule: A Translation and Commentary* (Collegeville, MN: Liturgical Press, 1996), 240.

The same idea is repeated in the description of how all who are called to serve in a special way are to act. The deans exercise care for their groups of ten (21.2), and the cellarer must show care for the sick, children, guests, and the poor (31.9). In fact, the cellarer is to take care of everything, of all that the abbot entrusts to him (31.5, 15). Care of the sick is to rank above and before all else (36.1, 6, 7, 10), and great care is to be shown in receiving guests (53.15). Those who exercise these special roles are themselves to be cared for—the cellarer, the porter, the kitchen servers (31.17; 66.5; 35.3, 4). Sometimes this is to be shown by the fact that they are given extra help when their task is burdensome, and sometimes, as with the kitchen servers, they are to be given some food or drink before they serve to enable them to carry out their tasks without undue pressure.

b) Wisdom and Fear of the Lord

The basis for the community's choice of abbot is that they should discern in him goodness of life and wisdom in teaching (64.2). This is the sort of wisdom that comes from being steeped in the Word of God. Only from this comes wise teaching. It also comes from a true perception in those who exercise authority: that in all they do, they should depend on God. In his relationships the abbot must always exercise wisdom. He is to be a wise physician (27.2; 28.2), and out of such a loving relationship healing can happen. The virtue of wisdom is obviously very important for Benedict. The deans also are chosen for virtuous living and wise teaching (21.4). The cellarer is to be someone who is wise and mature (31.2), the porter is to be a wise old man (66.1), and the house of God is to be in the care of wise men who will manage it wisely (53.22).

All who exercise authority will act wisely if the basis of their action is fear of the Lord, another very important characteristic for Benedict. They will acknowledge the presence of God in their own and in others' lives, and thus they will act in humility and wisdom. We are told that the abbot must fear God (3.1), and that he is always to be fearful of the future examination by the Shepherd (2.40). He will, however, always be well aware that those who fear God lack nothing (2.36). A healthy attitude toward this fear of the Lord will lead those who exercise responsibility to know that they must render an account to God for their service. Indeed, they must be worthy of the trust that has been given to them, knowing that more is required from those to whom more has been given (2.30; Luke 12:48). The idea that the abbot is to be worthy of his calling is repeated often (2.6-7, 34, 37-40; 64.7). He is to be a worthy steward.

The community likewise will act in the fear of God, particularly in their choice of abbot (64.1). The cellarer is to be God-fearing (31.2), and the sick are to be served by someone who is God-fearing (36.7). Those who deal with the guests will also be characterized by this virtue. The guests are to be entrusted to a God-fearing brother (52.21), and the porter is to act with all the gentleness that comes from the fear of God (66.4). In this atmosphere of wise and humble relationships, perfect love, which has no place for fear in its negative sense, will flourish (1 John 4:18).

What Effect Will This Have?

If such virtues are evident in the abbot and those who hold special places of service in the community, their modes of operation clearly will be affected. The basic attitude that authority is a call to serve in love will affect all decisions and relationships in the community. The abbot's behavior will always be reflective, flowing from a life of mindfulness of God, of others, and of his own role. And since he knows his own frailty, this will affect his attitudes and judgments of others. He will never act without depending on the wisdom of members of the community, in whom he knows the Spirit of God resides.

a) A Spirit of Service

The abbot, aware that prestige or privilege is never part of his office, undertakes his role in a spirit of service. He knows he is to remember that he is called "lord" and "abbot" not out of any claim of his own but out of consideration for Christ. This leads to an emptying of self in utmost service, as with the Christ who washed the disciples' feet (John 13). Thus does the abbot fulfill the Gospel teaching, "You know that the rulers of the Gentiles lord it over them, and their great ones are tyrants over them. It will not be so among you" (Matt 20:25). A spirit of service is evident as the abbot endeavors to serve a variety of temperaments (2.31). This surely requires utter selflessness; but when he has ministered well he can expect the Lord to reward him (64.21).

The abbot, who has been called from the community into this special role of service, has learned to serve in a community where all are to serve one another, and in love (35.1, 6). The spirit of service is also evident in the one who is called to serve the sick (36.7, 10), and also in the cellarer, who is expected to serve well (31.9).

b) Mindfulness and Reflection

Memor and *cogitare* are words often used to remind the abbot how he must behave. He has to think seriously about his duty, remember God, and thus act in a spirit of mindfulness and reflectiveness. In particular he is to remember what he is and what his title signifies and to what he is called (2.1, 30). As a "father" (with all the connotations of the desert tradition of teaching and giving life that this word bears), the abbot will be well aware of his life-giving role. That he is always to remember the judgment of God is a frequent theme, and reflection on this aspect of his calling will ensure that he acts fairly and compassionately. He has to remember never to crush the bruised reed (64.13). The thing that will help him to keep focused on his true role is that he will always strive to seek first the kingdom of God (2.35).

c) Awareness of Frailty

If the abbot is aware of his own frailty, it follows that such truthfulness and humility will certainly influence his behavior toward others. Benedict clearly states that he must always keep his own frailty before his eyes (64.13). This follows immediately after the prescription that, in correcting the vices of the brothers, he is to act prudently and avoid extremes, lest in trying too ardently to scrape off the rust, he break the vessel (64.12). Perhaps the use of *frangatur* in this phrase is a reference to the *fragilitas* of the next sentence. One who is humble enough to face his own weakness will certainly never judge harshly the weaknesses of others. This statement about the abbot also shows that though, at times, more than seems possible is expected of him, in fact he is simply struggling with his own limitations as are all members of the community. Mercy will always triumph over judgment as he treats each individual in ways that are for growth and life (2.16, 21-22; 64.10).

d) Discerning and Taking Counsel

It also follows that if the abbot and those in special positions in the community know their own limitations and act wisely and in an awareness of their responsibility, they will be able to draw on the wisdom of others, believing that all possess the Spirit of God. This is the basis of chapter 3, which notes that when anything important is to be done in the community, all are to be called to give counsel. Thus, all will be done for the health of the community.

Many words are used by Benedict to describe the attitudes that inform such an approach: *consilium, discernere, iudicare, pendere, discretio.* Discernment is to be exercised in the allotment of rank in the community (63.1). In assigning tasks, whether those tasks relate to God or the world, discernment and moderation are called for (64.16). In fact, he is to arrange everything so that the strong have something to yearn for and the weak are not frightened away (64.19). This discernment that leads to such moderation in action requires a careful pondering of possibilities. It requires that all who make decisions do not do so alone, but only after carefully seeking advice and pondering what has been heard. All of this informs the spirit of service the Rule requires. Such a spirit is the fruit of dialogue and mutual respect and can only come out of a life of reflection on the Scriptures.

Conclusion

Sometimes the members of the community are described as "souls," sometimes as "disciples," sometimes as "the weak," but most often as "brothers." This is the basis of all that Benedict says about the abbot and those in any position of authority. All of us are always worthy to be called brother or sister, and we all bear Christ to one another. In being called to his role in the community, the abbot knows this, and hence he can be and act in ways that are not turbulent, anxious, excessive, obstinate, jealous, or prone to suspicion (64.16). He holds the place of Christ in the community (2.2; 63.13), thus making Christ present in all that he is and does. But at all times he remembers that Christ is also present in the members of community, that they are struggling to cherish Christ above all, and that Christ will be found in the sick, in the guests, and in the daily circumstances of life. In all that the abbot does, he makes it possible for this to happen so that we will have a community united in seeking God.

5

Benedict's Abbot
and Saint Augustine

As we know, much of Benedict's Rule is not his original creation. One of his important sources is the Rule of Saint Augustine. The influence of Augustine's Rule is especially evident in the later chapters of the Benedictine Rule.

It is interesting to note the distinct change of "tone" in how Benedict regards the abbot when we compare chapter 2 of his Rule ("On the Qualities of the Abbot") with chapter 64 ("On the Election of an Abbot"). Chapter 27 ("On the Abbot's Concern for the Excommunicated") and chapter 28 ("On Those Who Refuse to Amend after Frequent Reproofs") also contain some important teaching on the abbot, and there are also distinct changes in these chapters. In fact, it seems there are important developments in the content or even profound differences between these latter chapters on the abbot and chapter 2. Chapter 2 is, with some important modifications, taken almost entirely from the Rule of the Master. There is a strong scriptural basis to chapters 27 and 28, and references there to Cyprian are most obvious. In chapter 64 there are references to Cyprian and also to Augustine. This latter chapter is full of the theme of compassion, and there is an emphasis on relationships and a greater awareness of the fragility of the abbot.

Benedict obviously believes strongly in the centrality of the abbot, and he gives very strong emphasis to this theme at the outset of the Rule. Furthermore, it seems likely that he wrote the Rule over a long period of time. This could explain the changing emphases. Experience taught him to emphasize strongly other significant aspects of community life as well, and so he may have felt the need to modify his original teaching. The only evidence that this is so would be the developments and modifications within the Rule. There is a phrase in chapter 59 (a very insignificant chapter "On the Offering of Sons by Nobles or by the Poor") warning that false expectations are not to be built up: "May God forbid this, but we have learned from experience that it can happen" (*quod experimento didicimus*, that is, "something we have learned by experience," 59.6). If one were to follow this line of argument, it would also be very significant to note what sources influenced Benedict. This is where we see his ample use of Augustine, both in quality and quantity. An article of Michael Casey's explores Benedict's use of Augustine and the change in emphases in Benedict's thinking that seems to have resulted from it.[1]

I now propose to examine the link between Augustine and Benedict with regard to the authority of the abbot or *praepositus*. In doing so, I will try to draw some implications regarding aspects of Benedict's teaching that could have resulted from the influence of Augustine.[2] I will pursue the topic in two sections:

---

[1] Michael Casey, "*Quod experimento didicimus*: The Heuristic Wisdom of St. Benedict," *Tjurunga* 48 (May, 1995): 3–22. See also Adalbert de Vogüé, *Community and Abbot in the Rule of Saint Benedict*, vol. 1 (Kalamazoo, MI: Cistercian Publications, 1979), 89. Here the point is made that, in comparing texts, care must be taken because Augustine and Benedict would both have used some of the same sources. Therefore, one cannot assume that similarities between them derive solely from Benedict's use of Augustine.

[2] Claude Peifer says that the second most important influence on Benedict after the Master is Saint Augustine. He notes that from

In a first section I will examine the texts from Augustine that appear in chapters 2 and 64 of the Rule of Benedict; and then, in a second section, I will attempt to achieve a comparative view of the structures of their two Rules and the position occupied in these Rules by the teaching on the abbot or *praepositus* and the community.

Section 1. Textual Comparisons

The main source for chapter 2 of the Rule of Benedict, "On the Qualities of the Abbot," is the Rule of the Master. Except for a few modifications, Benedict's text here repeats the material from his source almost word for word. There are only two references to Augustine in this chapter 2 of the Rule, and they relate to the notion of the abbot's responsibility and accountability for his charges. There is a reminder to the abbot not to be concerned with the fleeting things of this world to the extent that he thereby neglects the welfare of those entrusted to him (2.33). Augustine had used the same words as Benedict does here: *rebus transitoriis et terrenis* ("things fleeting and temporal").[3] Of course, both may be an echo of 1 John 2:17 (*et mundus transit*, "and the world is passing away"). More significant is the phrase Benedict uses in both chapter 2 and chapter 64: *rationem redditurus est* ("he must give account," 2.34; 64.7), with the same meaning as Augustine's use of it[4]: the responsibility and accountability of the one in charge of a community.

Augustine comes "the humaneness and concern for fraternal relationships" in the Rule (*RB 1980*, 64). De Vogüé in turn comments that, partly under the influence of Augustine, Benedict is interested in the monks' individual differences, their innermost feelings, and their mutual relationships. See Adalbert De Vogüé, *The Rule of Saint Benedict: A Doctrinal and Spiritual Commentary* (Kalamazoo, MI: Cistercian Publications, 1983), 198.

[3] Augustine, *Sermo* 113.6.

[4] Augustine, *Epistula* 211.15.

The connections with Augustine are more significant and numerous in chapter 64. Augustine's referenced texts are part of the reason for the tone of moderation and discretion and concern for the community which pervades this chapter. I also believe that this helps to give the chapter a more community-oriented approach, contrasting the very abbot-centered approach of chapter 2.

Three points emerge from a comparison of texts here: The first is that the abbot should fulfill his function in such a way that it is love rather than fear that informs his relationships with the community. As with Augustine, the abbot in Benedict is reminded that he, too, is subject to the Rule.[5] Benedict says: "Let him strive to be loved rather than feared"—*et studeat plus amari quam timeri* (64.15). Augustine's phrase is: *et quamvis utrumque sit necessarium, tamen plus a vobis amari adpetat quam timeri, semper cogitans deo se pro vobis redditura esse rationem*[6] ("although both are necessary, let her seek to be loved rather than feared by you, always keeping in mind that she is to render an account to God"). Augustine uses the notion of love rather than fear in connection with accountability, whereas Benedict uses it following the notion of the need to prune away faults with prudence and love as he sees what is best for each individual (64.14). Augustine also used this idea in writing to a monastery of nuns, reminding the prioress that she has to count herself happy not by exercising the power that rules but by practicing the love that serves. He then goes on to say that, in cheerfully observing and cautiously imposing rules, she is to be more anxious to be loved that feared—*tamen plus a vobis amari appetat quam timeri.*[7]

The second point I would like to pursue is that the abbot is to exercise his role in a spirit of service to the community and not

[5] *Rule of Augustine* 7.3. See RB 64.20.
[6] Augustine, *Epistula* 211.15.
[7] Augustine, *Epistula* 211.15.

for his own self-advancement. Benedict states that the abbot must make the benefit of his monks his goal, not preeminence for himself: *sciatque sibi oportere prodesse magis quam praeesse* (64.8). This is an echo of three different texts of Augustine. *Praeesse* ("to be in charge") and *prodesse* ("to be of benefit") are verbs used by Augustine when he is reflecting on his own role as a bishop.[8] In another text, Augustine comments that the task itself and not the honor of the position is important, and that the purpose of it all is the well-being of the people being served through authority: *debet enim, qui praeest populo, prius intellegere se servum esse multorum* ("for he who is in charge of people must first understand that he is the servant of many").[9]

The same point is made in a lengthy discussion about Rachel and Leah.[10] Here Augustine says that it is never the fact of being a leader that is important but rather the usefulness of the role. The action and business of leadership must be exercised solely for the public benefit, and indeed many will want to avoid such a laborious life exposed to so many common vicissitudes.

The third point is that the monks must be loved even if they fall. There are three references from Augustine that form a background for Benedict's teaching that the abbot must hate the faults of the brothers but love the brothers themselves: *oderit vitia, diligat fratres* (64.11).[11] There is a development of this idea in a text where Augustine notes that no matter how serious the sin, the sinner is never without hope. The passage ends with the phrase, *dilige hominem, oderis vitium* ("love the man, hate the vice").[12] The reference, however, is even clearer in the *City of God*, where Augustine says that the one who lives

---

[8] Augustine, *Sermo* 340.1. This sermon was given on the anniversary of his ordination as a bishop.

[9] Augustine, *De civitate Dei* 19.19.

[10] Augustine, *Contra Faustum* 25.56.

[11] Cf. Augustine, *Epistula* 211.11.

[12] Augustine, *Sermo* 49.5.

by God's standards must hate what is evil. He should not hate the person because of the fault, nor should he love the fault because of the person. He should hate the fault, but love the person: *sed oderit vitium, amet hominem.*[13]

These are all texts from chapter 64 of the Rule in which Benedict insists on the need to use love rather than fear in pruning away faults. In them he emphasizes the role of the abbot as existing for the good of the monks rather than the abbot's personal preeminence. Finally, great stress is laid on the need to love the monks even when there is evil in their actions. All of this marks a definite shift of emphasis in the envisioned relationship between the abbot and his community, and a stunning contrast to the tone of chapter 2.

Section 2. Structural Comparison of the Two Rules

We will no longer concern ourselves now with direct references to Augustine, but rather return to the suggestion I have made above that Benedict gradually learned a great deal from his own experience as abbot between the writing of chapters 2 and 64. I think it is possible that Augustine came to influence Benedict more and more in the latter part of the Rule as Benedict left behind the dominant influence of the Rule of the Master.

It is enlightening in this connection to compare the structure of the two Rules, that of Augustine and that of Benedict. In fact, Augustine's whole Rule exhibits a strong emphasis on community, and the opening phrases make this clear: "We urge you who form a religious community to put the following into practice. Before all else, live together in harmony, being of one mind and one heart on the way to God. For is it not precisely for this reason that you have come to live together?"[14]

---

[13] Augustine, *De Civitate Dei* 14.6.
[14] *The Rule of St. Augustine*, trans. Raymond Canning (London: Darton, Longman, and Todd, 1984), 1.1-2.

Until chapter 4, the Rule of Augustine is concerned with the place of individuals in the community, their aspirations, weaknesses, and sins. From here on, the Rule looks more at the life of the group as a whole.[15] In the first part, there is emphasis on the needs of individuals for food, clothing, care when sick, and even on the need to receive correction from others, since all are responsible for mutual correction. In the second part, we find the teaching on enduring love, mutual forgiveness, and the profound meaning of deep unity and love, something far more important than superficial uniformity. In this way the Rule moves to the heart of the matter. Love as a living factor within the relationships of a community is what makes explicit the fact that God is at the heart of the community's life.[16]

It is not until almost the end of Augustine's Rule, precisely in chapter 7, that the question of authority and obedience is treated. Even here the same warmth of relationships that has pervaded the Rule reappears. The monks are to obey their superior as a father, so his role is clearly more than that of a mere executive or social organizer. It is at this point that the Rule of Augustine uses the word *pater* for a single time, and this is accompanied by the first important use of a word for *obedience*. In the light of Augustine's understanding of the primacy of love, it seems that when love is the way, and unity of heart entirely centered on God is the goal, then obedience itself is above all concerned with personal relationships. The very significant Scripture texts the Rule uses here show that such an atmosphere of love and unity is what sets the tone for all relationships in the monastery: "Let [the monk] show himself an example to all in good works; he is to reprimand those who neglect their work, to give courage to those who are disheartened, to support the weak and to be patient with

---

[15] Agatha Mary, *The Rule of Augustine: An Essay in Understanding* (Villanova, PA: Augustinian Press, 1991), 13.
[16] Mary, 199.

everyone. In ready and loving obedience, the monks show
compassion to themselves, but also to their superior."[17] The
Rule then ends with a concluding exhortation in chapter 8, an
exhortation to live as free persons under grace and in such a
way as to spread abroad the living aroma of Christ.[18]

The Rule of Benedict, on the other hand, after the exhortation of the Prologue, which does express warmth by the
way it encourages the monk to seek God, moves on at once
in chapter 2 to the teaching on the abbot. The relationship of
the abbot to his monks as their teacher and shepherd is expressed warmly. Unlike Augustine, Benedict uses the word
abba with all the connotations of spiritual fatherhood that it
brings from the early desert and monastic tradition. Because
of the dominance of this usage, Benedict's use of *pater* does
not seem to emphasize so strongly the family relationships
that seem to be in Augustine's single use of that word: "Obey
your superior as a father."[19]

There is in Benedict a very early awareness of the importance of the community in chapter 3, "On Summoning the
Brothers for Counsel." Chapter 4, "On the Tools for Good
Works," also certainly provides many maxims that are necessary for living in the community in unity and love. When
compared with the emphasis of Augustine in the early parts
of his rule, however, we may say that Benedict is very "abbot-
centered." There is some modification of this in the shifting
emphases of some of the following chapters. Monks other
than the abbot, for instance, are also seen to exercise authority.
There is mention of deans and seniors in chapter 21, "On the
Deans of the Monastery," and in chapter 22, "On the Sleeping
Arrangements of the Monks." Older and wiser monks help
when there is need to exclude someone from the community,

[17] RA 7.14. Cf. Tit 2:7 and 1 Thess 5:14.
[18] RA 8.1.
[19] RA 7.1.

as called for in chapter 27. Attitudes of warmth and the need for good relationships are mentioned in chapter 31, "On the Qualifications of the Monastery Cellarer." In chapter 35, "On the Kitchen Servers of the Week," a strong notion of mutual service and love is communicated: "Let all the rest serve one another in love" (35.6). There is the same emphasis also in chapter 36, "On the Sick Brothers," which prescribes that the sick are to be cared for with every attentiveness.

But differences in tone strike the reader by the time Benedict comes to chapter 64, "On the Election of the Abbot." It is as if a gradual shift and modification have taken place in the understanding of the abbot's role. Then, from chapters 68 to 72, there is a distinct change in emphasis. In these particular chapters, community relationships and concern for individuals are paramount. The key chapters in this respect are chapters 71, "On Mutual Obedience," and 72, "On the Good Zeal of Monks." After the very "vertical" notion of obedience proposed in the early chapters of the Rule, it is more than surprising to find in chapter 71 a statement such as this: "Obedience is a blessing to be shown by all, not only to the abbot but also to one another as brothers, since we know that it is by this way of obedience that we go to God" (71.1). The phrase "by this way of obedience"—*per hanc oboedientiae viam*—now includes the obedience to one another: *sed etiam sibi invicem ita oboediant fratres* ("but let the brothers also obey one another in this way").

Even if Benedict had said nothing else throughout the Rule on mutual, loving relationships until chapter 72, however, what he says here would be more than adequate to show how important he thought these relationships were. Though this chapter comes at the end of the Rule, it is written with the same conviction and passion with which Augustine speaks of the need for loving relationships. The Latin vocabulary for "love" is here almost exhausted by Benedict, and with superlative modifiers: *zelum ferventissimo amore exerceant, caritatem fraternitatis impendant, amore Deum timeant, abbatem caritate diligant* (72.3, 8-10). The complete self-forgetfulness that love demands comes to the fore, as do respect for others and the need for patience and the support of weakness (72.4, 5, 7).

There are two significant instances of Augustine's influence in chapters 71 and 72 of the Rule, where Benedict finally expresses a deep understanding of the importance of mutual relations in community living. The first is the phrase he uses in chapter 71, "On Mutual Obedience," where, like Augustine, he speaks of *oboedientiae bonum* ("the good of obedience"); (71.1).[20] Then comes a reflection of Augustine's insight that only if Christ is the center of the individual monk's and the community's life can this life be truly lived. It occurs in Benedict's use of the phrase *et nihil praeponat Christo*, from Augustine's *Commentary on Psalm 29*, which Benedict introduces at the end of his exhortation to mutual love in the formulation *Christo omnino nihil praeponant* ("let them prefer nothing whatever to Christ"); (72.11).

When de Vogüé is discussing how the role of the deans (or officials) seems to have lost importance as the Rule progresses, he notes that the two pillars of Benedict's teaching are the community and the abbot: "Insistence on the authority and responsibility of the abbot, on the one hand, and on fraternal relations, on the other: this twofold accent seems to have entailed a lessening of the attention previously given to the subordinate officers, the deans."[21] Community and superior are indeed the pillars for Augustine as well. But as the above discussion has shown that not only do some of the officials lose their importance but also that the balance and the emphasis in how the two writers saw community and abbot or *praepositus* are very different. This is not to imply that Benedict did not see the abbot's role as a central factor in his teaching. The more one studies the Rule, the more one sees just how

---

[20] Augustine, *De Civitate Dei* 13.20.
[21] De Vogüé, *Rule of Saint Benedict*, 173.

important the abbot is. I believe, however, that it is not too much to presume that Benedict learned by experience the great significance of communal relationships, and so modified his teaching on the role of the abbot in the light of this, having been strongly influenced by the work of Augustine.

6

Taking Counsel

A Search for Wisdom

GOOD MANAGEMENT THEORY WOULD acknowledge the importance of involving the entire organization in important decisions that affect the whole. It seems obvious that it is prudent
to maintain good communications so that all members are
aware of what is happening. Thus are dissension and alienation prevented and all are able to "own" what is decided.
It is also acknowledged that members are able to contribute
to the decision-making process out of their experience and
knowledge. Better decisions will then result for the greater
benefit of the whole. Most organizations endeavor to promote
dialogue between management and labor so that high-quality
work will result.

Benedict in his time knew the value of consultation and
involvement, but his motivation, processes, and basic beliefs
may have been very different. He understood that the Spirit
resides in every member of the community, and that wisdom
is to be sought from all, including the youngest member. Faith
in this guiding Spirit is the important dimension here.

An obtuse and nondiscerning stance is foreign to Benedict's
way of acting, as is evident in chapter 3 of the Rule, "On Summoning the Brothers for Counsel." He is not talking about
good-management theory. An examination of this chapter
shows that decisions that are made in the community are to
be made in the end by the abbot, but only after careful listen-

ing and discernment. It is a question of an exercise in faith and not a political ploy. Indeed, in other parts of the Rule we see clearly that the role of the abbot is never absolute, as for instance in chapter 63: "The abbot should not disturb the flock committed to him, nor should he arrange anything unjustly as if he had unlimited power" (63.2).

There is an important text in chapter 65, "On The Prior of the Monastery," which could be seen as a model for decision making in the community: "But if local conditions call for it, or the community makes a reasonable and humble request, and the abbot judges it best, then let him, with the advice of God-fearing brothers, choose the man he wants and himself make him his prior" (65.14-15). There are many elements expressed here as parts of the process of choosing a prior that can be seen as defining the path of good decision making. There are local circumstances which may call for particular examination and flexibility. There is the request of the community, made reasonably and humbly. And there is the fact that in the end it is the abbot alone that makes the decision, but only after receiving advice.

These elements are strongly present in chapter 3. Even the repetition of significant words is a factor expressing what is behind the process. There is no doubt that the whole community is to be involved with regard to all significant matters. The word *omnes* (or its derivatives) is used seven times in this very small chapter. All are to be called together on matters of importance (v. 1); if all are present this makes it possible for even the younger members to speak (v. 3); all are to follow the Rule in all things (v. 7); all things are to be done in the fear of God, and the abbot must render to God an account for all his decisions (v. 11); finally, all things are to be done with counsel (v. 13).

The word *consilium* is used five times in this chapter (vv. 2-4, 12-13), so it is clear that the idea of the abbot seeking advice and the brothers giving it is emphasized throughout. Derivatives of *praesumere* are used to indicate the attitude that should be present as the monks give their counsel. The community members cannot presume to assert their views boldly (v. 4). They are never to presume to argue with the abbot or with those outside the monastery (v. 9). Indeed, if they presume to do so, they are to be disciplined (v. 10). There is a sense here that, although each member must give advice, there is never to be the presumption that all wisdom is held by only one person.

The Roles

The roles played in the process are clearly described in chapter 3. The abbot is the key person. He first is to convene the whole community, and then tell them what is involved whenever important questions are to be decided (v. 1). He is to hear others' advice, ponder it, and then act in the way he thinks best (v. 2). The word *tractet* suggests that the process of pondering need not be easy. The truth can be drawn out or "extracted" only with some effort. The abbot then makes the judgment (v. 5), weighing up and judging what he has heard, and for this judgment he is accountable to God (v. 11). In less important matters he uses the counsel of the seniors only (v. 12). The key revelation of the abbot's role here is that on all matters, whether important and less important, he never acts without advice. It is assumed that he has the wisdom to distinguish the importance of different matters and, therefore, to determine whose advice he is to seek. In the end, however, it is he who must make the decision.

The role of all the community, or of the council of the seniors in less important matters, is simply defined as that of giving advice. Benedict also firmly states that the younger members are to be part of this process (3.3). This prescription is also repeated and expanded in chapter 63, "On Rank in the Community." We are here reminded, in connection with community rank, that in no situation at all should chronological age determine or influence order in the community: "After all, Samuel and Daniel judged the priests when they were just boys" (63.6; 1 Sam 3; Dan 13:44-62). It is not surprising, then, that Benedict wanted the advice of younger members to be given, since, as with Samuel and Daniel, the Lord may reveal what is best to the younger ones. Again, the faith element is to be noted. All are to obey when the decision is made, and all, including the abbot, are to follow the Rule in all things (3.7, 11). Thus, with the Rule as the guide, any possible thought that "anything goes" is avoided. The abbot who listens to advice, and the community members who give it, are always accountable to the Rule.

The Qualities

The qualities all are to exhibit in their actions take the process far beyond decision making in organizational terms. The abbot is to act with foresight and justice (3.6) and always in the fear of God and the observance of the Rule (3.11). On the other hand, the community members are to obey as befits disciples (3.6). They are to offer their advice with deference and humility and not assert their views in a bold manner (3.4), nor are they to argue impudently (3.9). The picture is built up by the use of strong words, such as *procaciter defendere* (v. 4), *proterve* and *contendere* (v. 9). Above all—and perhaps this is the strongest advice of all—no one, neither the abbot nor any community member, is to be so self-willed as to simply follow a personal agenda. Ultimately, the outcome will be what is for the health of the community. The word *salubrius* (3.5) also has an element of what is for the salvation of the community: here again we are plainly in the realm of faith.

Some Implications

Throughout chapter 3 there is that strong sense of mutuality which is then evident as well throughout the whole Rule. We see interactions between abbot and community, community

and abbot, abbot and God, and at all times among community
members, abbot, and the Rule itself. In fact, it is clear that the
single, constant factor influencing all judgments made is the
Rule. An assumption can also be made that in all these inter-
relationships among community, abbot, and Rule, there is at
all times an underlying sense of trust. The abbot obviously
believes that the opinion of the community (the conventual
chapter) is worthy of being heard. The community, for its part,
trusts that the abbot, after hearing its advice, will draw out
the truth carefully, that he will come to see the best decision
through the process of careful discernment.

When the community is called together for consultation,
the abbot must begin the process in a situation in which he
genuinely does not yet know the answer. He will never say,
"We will consult, but . . ." and then go about his business
already knowing what the outcome will be. This genuine
stance of not knowing the outcome presupposes an understanding that the Holy Spirit can work through all members
and through the process itself, and that the wisdom of all is
valuable. The abbot has to gather the facts and the advice of
others through a real process of discernment. If this is genuine,
all can rest in confidence that the decision will have been
made by a person who is daily listening to God's Word and
is therefore open to the Spirit in the particular circumstances
under discussion. So, too, ought each community member be
completely open to God's Word. Only within such a situation
will true discernment take place.

Discussions about structures of government often concen-
trate on hierarchical order. Perhaps more emphasis should
be given instead to trying to work out the best processes for
the giving and taking of counsel. It is important not to stifle
creativity through excessive filtering.

The practices of discernment and of discretion are often
linked by Benedict. It is this that enables Benedict to be discerning and moderate when assigning tasks, and it is these
same qualities that help the abbot to arrange everything so

that the strong are challenged and the feeble are not overwhelmed (64.17-19). Only someone with a listening heart can make such decisions. The abbot also needs to be able to discern the order or rank that each will hold in the community (64.16), and he brings his prayerful, thoughtful, and careful judgment to bear at all times, so as to be able to bring forth things both old and new (64.9). Benedict notes here that, in order to do this, the abbot must be learned in the divine law.

Something that can prevent a genuine process of taking counsel from occurring can be a time-conditioned factor: namely, the need or desire to come to a decision too quickly. It may be believed, for instance, that swift action is called for, especially if the outcome is thought to be known even before counsel is sought. The whole process of sifting and discerning that is called for in the decision-making process, however, can take a very long time, as do most things of importance. One often hears talk that confuses the discernment process with that of decision making. The latter should be the outcome of the discernment that precedes it. Discernment often requires further consultation and refinement before it can be clearly seen what the outcome ought to be. There needs to be careful listening and then further consultation, a back-and-forth process that may need to go on for a long time.

Another difficulty can be the feeling of inertia and alienation that can set in, preventing the community from offering advice. It can be much easier not to be involved, especially if the situation is a difficult one. A common enough comment is that the community has elected a superior and a council to make decisions, and that we must trust them to go ahead with it. This comment completely misses the point of what Benedict is saying. Indeed, on some matters the council must act alone, and generally what these matters are is spelt out in the different particular Constitutions. But apart from this, those in authority must believe that each member of the chapter is a holder of wisdom, and they must work to find ways by which that wisdom becomes available and is actually offered.

A community can also become alienated when the members feel that the asking of advice is simply a token *pro forma* procedure after the decision has already been reached. People rightly see this as an effort to try to make them "own" a decision, the making of which they actually had no part in. The community in such a case quickly becomes aware that the wise advice they could offer is not really required. Along such a path, relationships can become impoverished and the decisions made will almost surely be less than satisfactory. It is difficult to maintain the faith dimension of the community's life in such circumstances, though it must also be recognized that faith can grow through failure and mistakes as well. What a community should be able to hope for is that as much genuine effort as possible be given to this aspect of its life. After all, the outcome of decisions about matters of importance will affect each member's life.

Those in authority asking counsel must always give as much information as is needed by the community members in order to provide intelligent counsel. Partial information prevents wise advice being given. Those giving counsel must search their hearts to discover if such things as fear, prejudice, fear of change, or narrowness of mind are preventing true openness to the Spirit.

Benedict knew the destructive power of murmuring, and he condemns it is the strongest of terms, whether the murmuring occurs on the lips or in the heart (5.17). We are admonished that above everything else we are to refrain from murmuring (40.9). It is an evil that can erode the community's life (34.6). Yet in spite of such strong condemnation, Benedict notes in his great humanness that the kitchen servers are to be given an extra allowance of food and drink before serving, so that they may serve without murmuring (35.12-13). When he is making further prescriptions about community meals, Benedict adds the phrase, "And he is similarly to adjust and dispose everything so that souls may be saved and the brothers may perform their activities without any justifiable murmuring" (41.5). Surely, "justifiable murmuring" in the community could certainly be avoided if all the members were genuinely able to offer the wisdom of their experience in decisions that affect the life of the whole community. We speak, after all, of a "wisdom" that is acquired from a lifetime of listening to the Word of God.

In his commentary on the Rule, Terrence Kardong notes that chapter 3 is a very careful sketch of the kind of dialogue that must characterize a healthy cenobitic existence.[1] This seems a very true statement, and if it is accepted at face value, it behooves us to work to find the best possible ways by which all members of the conventual chapter are involved in the giving and taking of counsel. There are obligations that those in authority must assume, and there are attitudes and obligations that community members must assume. In the end, we must have faith in ourselves that we can be open to the Spirit; we must have faith in each other that each member is honestly trying to listen to the Spirit; and, above all, we must have faith in the Spirit's power to guide us. All of this will result in finally discovering what is for the salvation and health of the total community.

[1] Terrence Kardong, *Benedict's Rule: A Translation and Commentary* (Collegeville, MN: Liturgical Press, 1996), 76.

7

"Lay Aside Everything"

THERE IS NO DOUBT ABOUT THE primacy with which Benedict invests the Divine Office, the Work of God. The opening verses in chapter 43 of the Rule give an indication of this. The phrase "nothing is to be preferred to the Work of God" (43.3) is often quoted and sometimes misinterpreted. In the context of the opening verse of this chapter, it seems clear that Benedict means we are not to give priority to other things in relation to this call to prayer: "At the hour for the Divine Office, as soon as the signal is heard, he is to lay aside everything he is doing with his hands and hasten with all speed" (43.1). The passage reflects an attitude of eagerness for this prayer, which is what makes such "hastening" possible. This eagerness is one of the criteria which shows that the novice is truly seeking God (58.7).

Chapters 8–20 of the Rule of Benedict contain his main teaching on prayer. These chapters could very easily be dismissed because of the greatly detailed elaborations and prescriptions for liturgical prayer, many of which are no longer applicable today if taken literally. It would probably be safe to say that these chapters would not often be read by individuals, and that they are only heard during the public reading of the Rule. As with any ancient text, however, a close reading reveals many important principles that are as relevant today as they were in the sixth century.

Sacrosanctum Concilium, the Constitution on the Sacred Liturgy of the Second Vatican Council, provides many interesting insights that can keep the reader alert to some of the points that Benedict raised many centuries before. This document deals with the nature of the sacred liturgy and its importance in the Church's life. The Rule of Benedict also describes the nature of the liturgy and its absolute centrality in the monastic life.

It is not necessary to look for a structure or a development in these chapters of the Rule. We do not know whether Benedict even thought in such a structured way. We must beware of reading things back into a text from today's perspective. An examination of the chapter headings, however, does show some development and interconnection among them, and it is worthwhile to take a look at their general outline before examining their content.

Chapters 8–15 deal with details for the celebration of Vigils and Matins. Chapters 16–18 deal with the day hours. Chapters 19 and 20 speak of the attitudes that one brings to prayer. They strive to ensure that we do not make a dichotomy between personal and liturgical prayer. Chapter 16 gives the rationale for the whole system: that this prayer is a prayer of praise and unifies our whole day. The psalm phrase "Seven times a day I praise you" (Ps 119:164) provides the theme that pervades the chapter and underlies Benedict's approach to liturgical prayer.

In the light of this we can group the chapters as follows:

Concerning Vigils and Matins

Chapter 8:	The Divine Office at Night
Chapter 9:	How Many Psalms Are Said at the Night Hours
Chapter 10:	How the Night Office Is to Be Celebrated in Summer
Chapter 11:	How Vigils Are Celebrated on Sunday
Chapter 12:	How the Solemn Office of Lauds Is to Be Celebrated

Liturgical Principles

a) An Integrated Approach

The first point one could draw from these chapters is that they describe an integrated approach to prayer and life. We are reminded of a statement in the *Sacrosanctum Concilium* which links personal prayer and liturgical prayer: "The divine office, because it is the public prayer of the Church, is a source of piety, and nourishment for personal prayer."[1] One could say that the reverse is true—personal prayer also nourishes liturgical prayer. So we are speaking not simply of prayer, but of a life of prayerfulness. The link is also made through the fact that the Word of God is central to personal prayer and it is also at the heart of the liturgy. "Sacred scripture is of the greatest importance in the celebration of the liturgy. For it is from scripture that lessons are read and explained in the homily, and psalms are sung; the prayers, collects, and litur-

---

[1] *Sacrosanctum Concilium* (The Constitution on the Sacred Liturgy), 90.

gical songs are scriptural in their inspiration and their force, and it is from the scriptures that actions and signs derive their meaning."[2] The document then goes on to speak of the need to develop a "warm and living love for scripture."[3]

Mary Collins notes that Benedict's admonition in the Prologue to "listen carefully . . . [and] attend . . . with the ear of your heart" (v. 1) in fact sets the theme for reflection on liturgical spirituality. We learn by heart the things we must do together in the liturgical assembly. We learn by heart in order to take to heart the saving mystery we celebrate. But learning by heart, listening with the ear of the heart, and taking to heart the mystery of Christ are the work of a lifetime, not a lesson to be mastered in a short course or a single day's participation.[4] Thus, our prayer is the work of a lifetime and it is fully integrated into whatever we do in our life. We are reminded of Cassian's approach to a life "when all love, all desire, all effort, all inclination, all our thought, all that we live, that we speak, that we breathe, will be God . . . , and that whatever we breathe, whatever we know, whatever we speak, would be God."[5]

Such an integrated approach to life, one in which liturgy and prayer are not separated from the ordinary activities, is truly sacramental. Benedict may not have used the word "sacramental" explicitly, but the connoted attitude is reflected in the text of the Rule over and over again. Through the ordinary events of life, God is revealed. A few examples will illustrate the point.

The well-known phrase "so that in everything God may be glorified" (57.9) occurs at the end of the chapter, "On the Artisans of the Monastery," an interesting fact in itself since it connects the ordinary work that we do with glorifying God.

---

[2] SC 24.

[3] SC 24.

[4] Mary Collins, *Contemplative Participation* (Collegeville, MN: Liturgical Press, 1990), 75.

[5] Cassian, *Conference* 10.7.2.

Cassian's recommended phrase from Psalm 70:1, "O God, come to my assistance,"[6] is used as the opening versicle for the Office when describing how the Psalms are to be sung in the Work of God during the day (17.3; 18.1). But it is also used by the kitchen servers as they begin their week of service (35.17). In the same way, the psalm phrase "O Lord, open my lips, and my mouth will declare your praise" (Ps 51:15) is used at Vigils (9.1), but it is also used by the reader as he begins his weekly service (38.4). Because of this attitude—which sees no dichotomy between what we normally think of as "sacred" and as "secular"—Benedict can state that the monk is "to look upon all the vessels as though they were the sacred vessels of the altar" (31.10). In the same breath he can speak of the kitchen servers washing the towels, the feet of the monks and the utensils, knowing that in all cases what is done is a service of Christ (35.8-10). This is why we must take such care of the material goods of the monastery (32.4).

Chapter 48 is another example of the complete integration of which Benedict is speaking. This chapter, "On the Daily Manual Labor," so orders the day that there is a balance between manual labor and sacred reading. Everything is to be done with proper measure (48.9). But it is not a matter of weighing one thing against another as in the balance of the scales. It is rather the balance of a dancer, with all aspects attuned to one another, so that a wonderful whole results. What is being presented is a way of life where the monk is totally open to God, whatever the activity in which he is engaged.

Chapter 16, "On How the Work of God is to be Celebrated during the Day," certainly gives the rationale for the hours of the Divine Office. The song of praise flows throughout the day, linking all activity. The idea of praise is repeated five times in the small chapter, which derives its teaching from the psalm phrase "Seven times a day have I praised you" (Ps 119:164).

---

[6] Cassian, *Conference* 10.9.2.

There are individual components in our lives: work, prayer, community, solitude, and relationships with God and others; but they only make sense as an integrated reality. Our life is to be a whole life of prayer, even though many different activities are part of it.

b) Placement of the Chapters

Chapters 8–20 appear in the Rule directly after the chapters which may be described as dealing with the specific spiritual aspects of the monastic way of life. In the light of the above, however, one should be wary of such categorization. The previous chapters have dealt with silence, humility, and obedience, and they call for attentive listening. Terrence Kardong suggests that in placing the chapters here, Benedict may have wished to prolong a similarly contemplative tone.[7] This is a very different choice of placement from the Master's, who has these chapters as 31–49 in his numbering, and they follow chapters dealing with the practical details of kitchen, food, meals, sleep, and excommunication. In Benedict it is clear that the chapters are instead related to the monk's *conversatio*, to how he sustains his way of life and achieves his goal. Benedict here is chiefly concerned about a change of heart. He urges us to remember God's Word, reflect on it, and decide what we must do.

c) Terms Used

Benedict uses many terms to describe what we now normally call the "Liturgy of the Hours." Many of the terms convey a sense of our own work or God's work within our way of life. Benedict speaks of the "Divine Office" (8; 16; 19.2) or of "service" (16; 18.24), and thus the idea is conveyed that this is a duty of our state, a certain obligation of our discipleship, the living out of which will lead us to God. The term *Opus Dei*

---

[7] Terrence Kardong, *Benedict's Rule: A Translation and Commentary* (Collegeville, MN: Liturgical Press, 1996), 212.

("Work of God") is not used in chapters 8–20, but it is used seventeen times altogether in the Rule.[8] It is thus seen by Benedict as a work we have to do; but it can also be seen as the work that God does in us as he brings about our transformation. For liturgical prayer, Benedict uses the Greek word *synaxis* or "assembly" (17.7), which emphasizes that we gather for this prayer as part of what we do as a community.

d) A Rhythm for Times and Seasons

Current liturgical language often refers to our communal prayer outside the Eucharist as the "Liturgy of the Hours."[9] The emphasis given here is that, as we have an innate need to mark the passage of time and seasons as expressed in the secular calendar, so too do we live this rhythm of times and seasons of our Christian lives by our celebration of this prayer. Thus we are making time holy[10]: "The Divine Office is devised so that the whole course of the day and night is made holy by the praises of God."[11] In the whole sweep of time, in the journey of our return to God, we live out the mystery of Christ, day in and day out, week in and week out, year in and year out, and throughout the recurring seasons. In chapter 8 of the Rule we hear what must be done in winter and summer. In chapter 10 we hear of night and day. In chapter 13 we note that different psalms are to be said to reflect the time of the day. We have the Alleluia to mark Easter (chap. 15) and we have the feasts of the saints (chap. 14). Benedict speaks of the night and of silence in chapter 42, and he notes the special place of

[8] The term *Opus Dei* is used in the following texts of the Rule: 7.63; 22.6, 8; 43.title, 3, 6, 10; 44.1, 7; 47.title, 1; 50.3; 52.2, 5; 58.7; 67.2, 3.

[9] The term used in *Sacrosanctum Concilium* is "Divine Office" (SC 83–101).

[10] See *Upon the Tradition 11*: "Of Time Made Holy: A Statement on the Liturgy of the Hours in the Lives of American Benedictine Sisters" (Madison, WI; March 5, 1978).

[11] SC 84.

Sunday (chap. 11). Often we speak of "ordinary time" in the calendar, but there is really nothing "ordinary" about ordinary time! It is really *ordinal* time, counted time, numbered time until Christ returns in glory. Thus liturgy marks time, shapes us, and leads us to the future. In this way we are gradually shaped and transformed by the power of the Word of God.

e) The Central Place of Psalmody

The Word of God is central in our personal prayer and in our prayer in common. Scripture readings are part of this prayer, and the Psalms are a transforming power when repeated over and over. We may have adapted to contemporary needs Benedict's careful disposition of the Psalms in the *Opus Dei*, but we never ignore the central place that the Psalms play in our prayer. *Sacrosanctum Concilium* expresses this by noting that all who pray this prayer are earnestly exhorted to attune their minds and their voices when praying it: "The better to achieve this, let them take steps to improve their understanding of the liturgy and of the bible, especially of the psalms."[12]

We see this principle in Benedict's prescriptions. Though the lessons are not to be read when the nights are short, the number of the psalms is always maintained (RB 10.1-2). If the monks arise late, readings and responsories may be shortened, but not the Psalms (11.12). Chapter 18, "In What Order the Psalms Are to Be Said," gives details of the arrangement of the Psalms so that the whole one hundred and fifty psalms are said each week (18.23). The psalm verse *Seven times a day have I praised you* (Ps 119:164) forms the basis for the structure of how the Work of God is to be said each day.

f) The Place of Ritual

Benedict also understood the place of ritual in the celebration of the Work of God. A true understanding of ritual presupposes

---

[12] SC 90.

that the meaning of the action and of the words is kept alive. Meaning is here enacted in a symbolic way that includes the participation of body, mind, and spirit. Whether we stand to praise or sit to listen attentively, or recite the Psalms alongside one another in an expression of mutuality, the meaning has to be attended to. *Sacrosanctum Concilium* notes that the Divine Office is to be fulfilled as perfectly as possible: "This refers not only to internal devotion of their minds but also to their external manner of celebration."[13]

Such an exhortation echoes Benedict's own prescriptions. He notes that at Vigils, after the third reading, all the monks are to rise from their places out of honor and reverence for the Holy Trinity (9.7). Thus, he has included a description of both the action and its meaning. Similarly, an implicit pact to forgive is enacted when Benedict notes that, at the end of the celebration of Vespers and Lauds, the Lord's Prayer is to be said aloud by the superior for all to hear, "because of the thorns of scandal which are likely to spring up: so that the brothers, by means of the promise they make in that prayer which says 'Forgive us as we forgive,' may purge themselves of this sort of vice" (13:12-13).

g) The Question of Adaptation

Sacrosanctum Concilium as a whole is itself a model of adaptation. The restoration and revision of the rites is undertaken "in order that the Divine Office may be better and more perfectly prayed in existing circumstances."[14] Throughout the document we see norms being given not in order to burden rigidly but to make it possible for the liturgy to be better celebrated. The clue to genuine adaptation is that, simultaneously, the tradition is respected and present circumstances are taken into consideration. The objective is never to make choices that

[13] SC 99.
[14] SC 87.

conform the liturgy to the latest fad. The only way this can be avoided is to require that those who make such adaptation must first know and be steeped in the tradition. Only then can adaptations be fruitfully made.

Benedict understood this well when he spoke of the need for discretion on the part of the abbot, who should consider that "if I drive my flocks too hard, they will all die in one day" (64.18; cf. Gen 33:13). A striking principle of adaptation by Benedict appears toward the end of his liturgical code (18.22). After making so many careful prescriptions, it is surprising to find him in the end saying: "Above all we emphasize that if this distribution of the Psalms is displeasing, one may order things differently as he judges better." He then presents the framework within which these changes can be made: "provided that the full complement of one hundred and fifty psalms is by all means carefully maintained every week, and that the series begins anew each Sunday at Vigils" (18.23).

There is evidence of both adaptation and compassion in Benedict's provision that the first psalm of Lauds is to be sung somewhat slowly so that all may be there in time for Psalm 51 (13.2). The same arrangement holds for Vigils. Psalm 95 is to be said quite slowly and deliberately so that all may be in time for the rest of the Work of God (43.4). Adaptations are made if the community is large. In that case the Psalms are to be sung with refrains; but if the community is smaller, the Psalms are sung straight through (17.6). What is done is always within reason (8.1, 4).

Conclusion

What *Sacrosanctum Concilium,* the great document of the Second Vatican Council on the liturgy, is doing in our time, and what Benedict was doing in his, was ensuring that those who live a particular way of life are living an integrated prayerful life which supports the person in the seeking of God. Benedict's principles have stood the test of time and, although the material arrangements and details for celebrating the Work of God may have changed, the fundamental points are always maintained. In the celebration of the *Opus Dei*, we are sanctifying time and praising God, thus fulfilling the prescription to "pray always."

8

Community Table and Eucharist

ONE OF THE CENTRAL ASPECTS OF Benedict's Rule is his emphasis on community. Indeed, the lifestyle that Benedict describes
is uncompromisingly cenobitic. There is no doubt that Benedict
wrote his Rule for those who were to live the cenobitic life, in
other words, those who were to live in community. This is
clear from the very first chapter in which Benedict describes
the four kinds of monks. There is the forthright description of
the cenobites as the ones who belong to a monastery where
they serve "under a rule and an abbot" (1.1-2). At the end of
the chapter, having discussed the other three kinds of monks,
Benedict sets out to write the Rule proper, drawing up a plan
for "the strong kind, the cenobites" (1.13). The word *cenobite* is
used for the third and final time in chapter 5, "On Obedience."
Here the cenobites are described as those living no longer by
their own judgment—that is, giving in to their own whims
and appetites—but rather as walking according to another's
decisions and directions and choosing to live in monasteries
and to have an abbot over them (5.12). This is strong teaching
that is basic to community living; and, of course, the rest of
the Rule will add more and more as to what living in community involves.

In a kind of negative image, Benedict's descriptions of the
other three kinds of monks in chapter 1 show precisely what

he values in the cenobite. The anchorites can live profitably in their eremitical manner only after having lived in community for a long time and learning self-reliance and experiencing mutual help. They have been formed by community living and have learned to grapple single-handedly with vices and faults. Only then can they live alone (1.3-5). Thus, Benedict assumes that it is the community that has taught the anchorites these necessary eremitical virtues. Likewise, by condemning the sarabaites for their aloofness, for cutting themselves off from what they would otherwise learn in the community, and for not living under a rule (1.6-9), Benedict shows that community life is a guiding and formative experience. Living in community ensures that those who do so will not be able to live according to their own will. Stability in a community is required in order to live the Gospel. The gyrovagues clearly do not live this way (1.10-11).

All of this emphasizes the mutual support and the transformation that occur in the context of the community. Living the Christian life is more than one action or even a series of actions. It is a wholehearted commitment to a Gospel way of life in response to a baptismal call. So, too, is living in community. It is a total way of life in response to an initial call.

Community and Eucharist

a) Call and Response

Some aspects of our community life can be seen in parallel to aspects of eucharistic theology. In the Eucharist, we are strengthened and challenged to live more deeply the original baptismal call. Our response to baptism is to be one of lifelong fidelity to the Christian way of life.

The call of Benedictines is to live the Christian life in a particular way by undertaking a commitment to living according to the way of life Benedict sets out in the Rule. This is expressed clearly and urgently in the Prologue: "Therefore let us rise at long last, for Scripture stirs us with the words: 'It is high time we rose from sleep,'" and "'The Lord, seeking a worker for himself in the crowds to whom he cries out, says: 'Which of you desires life and longs to see good days?'" (Prol. 8, 14-15). The response to this call is described in the commitment made in chapter 58. After long testing, the new community member has promised stability, fidelity to the monastic lifestyle, and obedience, and the community has responded and committed itself to the new member in the threefold response to the *Suscipe*. The new member expresses this commitment in a total giving of self, keeping nothing and no longer having power even over his own body (58.17, 22, 24-25). Nothing could be more total than this.

b) Transformation

Growth and transformation in Christ take place throughout our lives. The Eucharist is the key transforming experience of our Christian life. Through it we are constantly challenged to live the Gospel, and the transforming power of God's Word becomes effective through it. We become the Body of Christ.

The Benedictine, pondering God's Word daily, and becoming one gradually with the body of the community, is transformed into Christ. Thus is the promise of the Prologue fulfilled: "As we progress in the monastic life and in faith, our hearts will swell with the unspeakable sweetness of love, enabling us to race along the way of God's commandments" (Prol. 49). This happens as we live out faithfully in community our response to the call of God.

c) Service

This fidelity is expressed specifically in the way Christians serve one another. Living out the eucharistic commitment demands this. Our experience in the eucharistic celebration must overflow in the way we serve one another, especially those who are in need. We come to see Christ in one another.

Benedict expresses this over and over as he calls his followers to service. Benedict's teaching on this matter becomes amply clear in the great eucharistic symbol of the table. Chapter 35, "On the Weekly Kitchen Servers," begins with the clear statement, "The brothers should serve one another" (35.1), and this is expanded on a few verses later. All who have no other commitments that would prevent such service "should serve one another in love" (35.6). The symbol of the washing of the feet, which graphically takes us back to Christ's gesture of self-giving on Holy Thursday, is also included. In answer to Basil's questions, "Whose feet will you wash? Whom will you serve?"[1] Benedict makes clear that we are to wash one another's feet, whether literally or symbolically, in service and mutual obedience. Just as the Eucharist makes sacred all our lives, so it is clear that our service of one another at meals ought to be performed with lives of total commitment. Prayer begins and ends the week of service, and such service is launched with the same prayer as is used at the beginning of most hours of the *Opus Dei*: "O God come to my assistance; Lord hasten to help me!" (35.17).

The sick are to be served within the community, and this service is to be valued above all else (36.1). As in the case of guests, it is Christ who is being served in them (53.1). In chapter 53, when the guests are received, the washing of the feet is again prescribed. The abbot as well as the whole congregation should wash the feet of all guests (53.13). Here the symbol is even clearer, since it is the abbot, he who holds the place of Christ in the community, who is to wash the feet of the guests. The table of the guests is likewise very important, and someone is appointed to ensure that the guests are fed well (53.16). Service also extends to ensuring that the beds are

---

[1] Basil of Caesarea in Augustine Holmes, *A Life Pleasing to God: The Spirituality of the Rules of St Basil* (London: Darton, Longman, and Todd, 2000), 139 ("Longer Rule 7").

made up for the guests (53.22). In the end, as in our gathering for Eucharist, strangers should become part of the body of the community.

d) Weakness and Forgiveness

As we grow together as members of the eucharistic community, we become aware of human weaknesses in one another. From this flows the need for forgiveness. We come to celebrate Eucharist as the sinners we are, and we hope to experience forgiveness. The celebration is not only for the perfect.

Benedict devotes many chapters of the Rule to his description of what is to be done when weaknesses and faults emerge among community members (23–30). He proposes exclusion and various means of bringing about the conversion of the erring ones. All the efforts are toward healing. This is exactly what we hope will happen when we celebrate Eucharist.

e) Silence and Solitude

We pray together as a community at Eucharist, but there is also the need to experience some silence and solitude as we relate to our God. We find God in this solitary way as well as in one another. Solitude and silence are necessary in our search for God in community, and there is no dichotomy between them and our service of one another. The two aspects interact and are parts of a whole. This truth is beautifully illustrated in a book on Iris Murdoch written by her husband, John Bayley. He describes the beginning of their marriage: "So married life began. And the joys of solitude. No contradiction was involved. The one went perfectly with the other. To feel oneself held and cherished and accompanied, and yet to be alone. To be closely and physically entwined, and yet feel solitude's friendly presence, as warm and undesolating as contiguity itself."[2]

---

[2] John Bayley, *Iris* (London: Abacus, 1998), 372.

Benedict, too, presents a healthy balance between the need for personal prayer and communal prayer. In the community he envisions, one is to find much silence wherein God can be found. Chapters 8–20 speak of the details of communal prayer and many important principles emerge here. We are to put nothing before our ready response to the call to prayer (43.1, 3). Chapter 6 speaks of the "intrinsic value of silence and the great importance of silence" (6.2-3). It is not by dint of much speaking that prayer is heard, but when it comes out of a pure heart and tearful compunction (20.3). These attitudes of the heart grow in silence, because here an honest appraisal of oneself can develop. Deepest silence is to follow the Work of God, and there is provision for those who wish to pray privately (52.2-4). Desire and full attention of the heart are also nourished in silence.

f) The Transcendent

The Eucharist is not just about the present. It looks toward the future and leads us toward what lies in the beyond. Through the powerful sensory symbols of the gathering of the assembly, the Word, the minister, and the elements of bread and wine, we are led to the eternal and the heavenly.

This influence toward the transcendent is also clear in the Rule. The embolism after the Our Father would have us "await the blessed hope and the coming of our Savior, Jesus Christ."[3] The focus of the Rule is that we live participating in the passion of Christ through patience so that we will deserve to be his companions in the kingdom (Prol. 50). We are to long for eternal life with the desire of the Spirit (4.46). When we have wielded the tools of the spiritual craft and returned them on Judgment Day, then we will receive the promised reward of the Lord: "What eye has not seen nor ear heard, God has

[3] *The Roman Missal, Third Edition* (Collegeville, MN: Liturgical Press, 2011).

prepared for those who love him (1 Cor 2:9)," (4.75-77). Those who long to attain the heavenly homeland, are those who carry out "this modest Rule for beginners" (73.8). From beginning to end, the transcendent element of the Rule is striking.

Community and Table

a) The Symbol of the Table

If we explore the great symbol of the table in the liturgy and in life as well as in the Rule, a great richness becomes apparent and the "eucharistic" connections of the Rule emerge. In most cultures, the table and the meal are key symbols of the unity of persons with one another. A detailed discussion of this theme may be found in an essay by Parker Palmer, in which he uses the idea of "staying at the table" as a symbol, suggesting that the practice expresses that to which members of a community are committed.[4] This powerful symbol recalls the utter self-giving of Christ to those who were about to betray him. It implies so much more than simple involvement and risk. In times of disillusionment, always inevitable when trying to live out any long-term relationship, we learn to rely more and more on God. Thus we can "stay at the table."

Whether we think of the table of the Last Supper and Jesus' utter self-giving there, or of the table of the Eucharist, or of the ordinary tables of our lives, there are many similarities among them.

b) A Place of Service

In the first place, the table is a place of service. At the Last Supper, after he had washed the feet of the disciples, Jesus

---

[4] Parker Palmer, "On Staying at the Table: A Spirituality of Christian Community," in *Pace* (Winona, MN: St. Mary's Press, 1984–1985), 2.

said: "Do you understand what I have done for you?" And then: "You call me 'Master' and 'Lord' and rightly so, for that is what I am. Then if I, your Lord and Master, have washed your feet, you also ought to wash one another's feet. I have set you an example: you are to do as I have done for you" (John 13:13-16). The ultimate gift of himself, symbolized in this gesture, was centered around the table for a meal. It was during supper that he rose from the table, girded himself, and washed the feet of the disciples.

There are surely echoes of these Gospel words in the following text on the abbot's call to service: "But the abbot, because we believe that he holds the place of Christ, is to be called 'lord' and 'abbot,' not for any claim of his own, but out of honor and love for Christ. He, for his part, must reflect on this, and in his behavior show himself worthy of such honor" (63.13-14). Such service is also echoed in Benedict's injunction to all: "Let us serve one another . . . Let us serve one another in love" (35.1, 6). It is at the table of the community that service such as this is most evident.

c) A Place Where Rituals Are Important

Rituals are important, as we see above all at the eucharistic table. Rituals enact the fact that we belong, and they also enhance this sense of belonging. As a community we do things in our own particular way, and if our ritual is to have meaning we should understand why we do it. Rituals show why we are together, and this meaning is expressed in the care we take and in the way we make the place of celebration beautiful. Familiar rituals which retain their meaning also allow one to rest comfortably into what is done. Engaging in ritual helps us to be more aware of the meaning of our actions.

Chapter 35 shows Benedict's understanding of the place of rituals in monastic life. He gives a prescription for the washing of towels, feet, and utensils, and for the giving out and receiving back of utensils (35.8-11). Nothing is considered unimportant. There is also the ritual blessing for those who are about to start their service, and the prescription that they should receive food and drink before their service. Both those beginning their service and those ending it are to ask the prayers of all after Sunday Lauds, bowing before the knees of all in the oratory. Particular words accompany these actions. Those ending their service thank God for helping them during the previous week, and those beginning the week ask for God's help. The rest of the community express their involvement and support by the threefold repetition of the prayers, and the blessing is then given (35.15-18).

There are also rituals attached to the reading at meals. The one who is to read for the week should ask the help of the community and of God, and he then receives a blessing (38.1-3). The reader is also to receive some wine before he carries out his task, and afterward he is to eat with the cooks and the servers, who have served in other ways during the meal (38.10-11).

The timing of the meals is also an important ritual. The prescriptions provide a regular structure for the day and also link the meals to seasons of the year and to the liturgical seasons (41).

d) A Place Where Needs Are Satisfied

Many needs are satisfied when one comes to the table. The need for nourishment—physical, psychological, spiritual—can be fulfilled at the table. Food will satisfy the body, and companionship and encouragement can assuage loneliness and provide support on the spiritual journey. We can experience this at the eucharistic gatherings and at the family table. We are nourished by the food of the Eucharist and the Word of God, and we are strengthened by one another in the assembly. At the family gatherings for meals, we experience a sense of identity, companionship, and support, as well as physical nourishment.

Benedict devotes three chapters to the details of the meals. It is interesting that the first of the three, chapter 38, deals with table reading. The hearers are admonished to be attentive, thus absorbing the spiritual edification (38.5). Only those who can read well are to read so that the hearers will be nourished as intended (38.12).

Physical nourishment is well provided for, and variety and substance are detailed regarding food and drink. There are special prescriptions for different seasons, places, and the amount of work undertaken (39.1-6; 40.5, 8). Arrangements also vary for the young and the sick (39.10-11; 40.3). Throughout these chapters there is acknowledgment that individuals are different from one another, and that their specific needs are to be attended to. "Each person is endowed by God with a special gift, some this, some that" (40.1; cf. 39.1).

e) A Place for Guests and Sharing

Guests are welcomed at the table, and this holds both for the eucharistic gathering and the family meal. No longer are these guests strangers. They entrust themselves to each other. In chapter 53 Benedict makes this clear, and its connections with chapter 35, "On the Kitchen Servers," are strong. The welcome is done out of love: "So, as soon as a guest is announced, the superior or the brothers should hurry to meet him with every mark of love" (53.3). The superior is to break his fast for the guests, and the kitchen is run by those who can do the task well (53.10, 17). Benedict's chapters "On the Exclusion of Erring Monks from the Table" emphasize the strong significance for him of sharing at table. He conveys the sense of complete isolation that results when a monk cannot eat with the others or even at the same time. This is almost the ultimate punishment (23–25).

f) The Community: A Sacrament

We normally speak of the "sacrament of the Eucharist." But here we are extending this concept and speaking as well of the sacrament of the table of our meals and of our lives. Here at this table we find Christ in each other. Just as we adore in the oratory (52), so too do we adore Christ in the guests who come, and in each other: "One must adore Christ in them, for he is in fact the one who is received" (53.7). We treat the food, each other, the table itself, and the setting as a reflection of the eucharistic table, which in fact they are. Benedict, who claimed that "we are to consider the pots of the monastery and all its goods as if they were the holy bowls of the altar" (31.10), understood this sacramental dimension of the "ordinary" in our lives. "[The cellarer] must not hold anything as negligible," he affirmed (31.11). Indeed, in these ordinary things—the table of our meals and the table of our lives, as well as in the table of the Eucharist—we find Christ and become a sign of Christ to each other. It is no wonder that the table is a central symbol of our community and links us closely to the table of the Holy Eucharist.

9

Looking Forward to Holy Easter

BENEDICT IS GIVEN TO WRITING PITHY opening sentences to his chapters—sentences that contain profound meaning. Many of these appear in the chapters that provide the context for chapter 49, "On the Observance of Lent." The openings of some of these chapters contain some wonderful comments on specific aspects of cenobitic life. In these opening declarations we read, for instance, that "monks ought to strive for silence at all times, but especially during the night hours" (42.1), and "at the time for the Divine Office, as soon as he hears the signal the monk should drop whatever is in hand and rush there with the greatest haste" (43.1). We also hear that "idleness is the soul's enemy, so therefore at determined times the brothers ought to be occupied with manual labor, and again at determined hours in *lectio divina*" (48.1). Finally we hear that "the oratory should be in fact what it is called and nothing else should be done or stored there" (52.1).

Lent and the Cenobitic Life

In the midst of these chapters and their strong opening statements, we are suddenly struck by the famous comment on Lent at the beginning of chapter 49: "At all times the lifestyle of a monk ought to have a Lenten quality." In his *Commentary*,

Terrence Kardong writes of chapter 49 as a gentle and serene approach to monastic life.[1] If we examine the chapter to find out in what ways this might be so, we will see that some of the ideas included in this chapter will naturally be linked to similar ideas appearing in other chapters that bear on aspects of the "internal organization of the cenobitic life."[2]

Benedict's own definition of cenobites as "those who live in monasteries and serve under a rule and an abbot" (1.2) comes fully to life in chapter 49. An individualistic accent prevails. The chapter begins in the singular: "The lifestyle of a monk ought to have a Lenten quality" (49.1). Then we are told that each one has to offer something extra to God beyond what is imposed, and that each one is to deny himself something and await Holy Easter with the joy of spiritual desire. Finally, each one is to propose an individual Lenten program to the abbot for his approval (49.6-8).

The communal element of Lent, however, is also clear in this chapter. Verses 2-5 are written in the plural. All should guard their lives with all purity and all should work together at effacing the negligences of other times. The use of *pariter* in verse 3 evokes the use of the same word in chapter 72.12. There the communal element is strong, as the monk is reminded that we will all be led *together* to life everlasting. We are urged to restrain ourselves from evil habits, to devote ourselves to prayer, reading, compunction, and asceticism. We are all encouraged to increase our measure of prayer and abstinence.

It is obviously good for a community to plan its Lenten observance together and to make sure that love and practical charity are part of this plan. The individual, however, has to make a full human response, a response from the inmost heart. The contest is enacted in the forum of the heart of each

---

[1] Terrence Kardong, *Benedict's Rule: A Translation and Commentary* (Collegeville, MN: Liturgical Press, 1996), 408.

[2] Kardong, 345.

person.[3] Thus, each person undertakes, of his or her own free will—but all together and with the abbot's approval—to respond to the call to conversion that is characteristic of the Church's celebration of Lent (49.3, 6, 8-10).

The Journey Theme

Liturgically and scripturally the theme of the Exodus is central to the celebration of Lent. The idea of the Israelites leaving the painful (yet at times secure) experiences of Egypt, spending time struggling in the desert, and finally arriving at the promised land, united as a people, is a constant liturgical theme of the season. This can be linked with the movement and journey theme in Benedict's Rule. The Prologue comes to mind immediately—the call, the aspects of the journey, the joy of arrival. The spirituality proposed is a dynamic one that leads to interior depth. In responding to God's energy, "the dynamic concepts of journey, movement and growth lead into the depths of the human heart, into God's innermost mystery and so into a deep solidarity with humanity."[4] We are reminded of the text from Hebrews, "By faith [Moses] left Egypt, because he had his eyes fixed on God's reward" (Heb 11:27).

The journey is one to be undertaken seriously, yet it is a joyful walk. The word *gaudium* is used only twice in the Rule (49.6-7). It is associated with the joy flowing from the unspeakable sweetness of love that is experienced as we progress in the way of life and in faith (Prol. 49). The path for the journey may remain narrow, but if our hearts are enlarged by love we see the journey differently. Such joy is the stimulation that enables us to begin the journey of conversion, to persevere in it, and finally to arrive at the goal of Easter. It is also that which enables us not only to walk but also to run on the

---

[3] Cassian, *Conference* 5.27.1.

[4] A. Böckmann, "Benedictine Mysticism: Dynamic Spirituality in the Rule of Benedict," *Tjurunga* 57 (1999): 85.

way of God's commandments. Running is more important than walking, as Benedict indicates, for example, when he changes the reference to John 12:35 in the earlier part of the Prologue from "walk while you have the light of life" to "run while you have the light of life" (Prol. 13). In this context we may be "running" lest darkness overtake us; but in chapter 49 there is always a sense of running *toward* something, full of the joy of spiritual desire. As we journey, there should be in us a spontaneous spirit of joyful love.[5] Then in joy we can offer something beyond what is expected or imposed (49.6).

A Journey of Reform

As in the great exodus from Egypt, the monk's journey, too, is a journey from death to life. As believers, we are always on the road of never completed Christian initiation; this is another reminder of the baptismal connections of the origins of Lent in the early Church. The Prologue demonstrates this by its use of Psalm 34 with its call and response as we set out on the path of conversion with the Gospel as our guide (Prol. 21). Lent is also a time of reconciliation as part of an interior conversion. It can take a long time and require a long walk to make this journey.

Lent calls us to reform ourselves individually as a community and as a Church. Christ's image should shine in us and in our communities more clearly as we respond to Benedict's challenge to amend our misdeeds (Prol. 36) or to change our evil ways (4.58). The hope that these may be healed, expressed at the end of disciplinary code, seems like a Lenten call for us to be renewed in sincerity and truth (30; Eph 4:24). The challenge is to change our ways of thinking, judging, and acting.

Traditionally prayer, fasting, and almsgiving have been thought of as the three chief practical aspects of our Lenten

---

[5] Kardong, 405.

conversion. Prayer and fasting are linked in chapter 49: "Therefore in these days we should increase the regular measure of our service in the form of special prayers and abstinence from food and drink, and let him deny his body some food, some drink, some sleep, some chatter, some joking" (49.5-7). This follows the call to devote ourselves to tearful prayer, reading, compunction of heart, and asceticism. Such prayer can come only from a deep awareness of who we are and what we could be. In the light of this awareness there arises in us an urgent and deep desire for change.

A Journey of Attentive Listening

Our transformation and conversion will only happen over a lifetime and will be wrought in us by our attentive listening to the Word of God. We are reminded of this by the call to devote ourselves to reading as well as to tearful prayer, compunction of heart, and asceticism (49.4). Perhaps the call is to intensify this devotion and thus live more faithfully what we always try to do in our daily *lectio divina* and in our attention to communally shared reading. In Lent, as in all liturgical seasons, the readings designated by the Church should be given particular attention since they are chosen to reflect the Lenten themes.

Chapter 48, which immediately precedes the chapter on Lent, gives special emphasis to the need for leisure or availability if we are to hear the Word of God that is spoken to us. While chapter 48 can generally be considered a description of how Benedict sees the monk's day, bringing into balance the various elements of his life, the word *vacet* (or its derivatives) is interwoven throughout the chapter. The monks must be free for *lectio divina* (48.4, 10); after the meal and in the mornings of Lent, they are to be free for readings and psalms (48.13-14); there is to be supervision when they are free for *lectio* (48.17); and on Sundays all should be free for *lectio* unless assigned to other tasks. The connection between freedom from other concerns, the idea of actively emptying oneself of other preoccupations, and hearing the Word of God, is surely not one of chance.

Such an attitude of availability and real leisure is fundamental to our attentiveness to the God who speaks to us daily. What we should do at all times, we do even more conscientiously in Lent. Thus there are "Sabbath moments" built into each of our days the year round; but, if we fail to take advantage of them faithfully and habitually, then the special call in Lent is not to fail to take such times-out in this holy season.

Only out of the silence can one hear, and so we are reminded to deny ourselves an excess of chatter and joking (49.7). In addition to other teaching on silence throughout the Rule, the chapters that provide immediate context for the chapter on Lent mention the idea of silence frequently. Silence and the night are connected in chapter 42, enjoining that "No One Is to Speak after Compline." The chapter conveys a sense of serious expectancy as one keeps vigil in the night. If the rule of silence is transgressed, there is to be a penalty (42.9). When the monks have a period of rest after their main meal, this is to be in total silence (48.5). And, in the reconciliation process after excommunication, the monk is to lie prostrate and silent outside the oratory. To hear what one must hear from God's Word, however it is spoken, requires silence.

A Journey of Desire

Benedict expresses very clearly the reason for our efforts as we make this Lenten journey: simply stated, we are awaiting Holy Easter with all the joy of spiritual desire (49.7). Here we have an echo of the phrase from earlier in the Rule, "to long for eternal life with the full desire of the spirit [*omni concupiscentia spiritali desiderare*]" (4.46). A great intensity of desire is expressed in this phrase. The desire meant here is a reaching out for what is to come, or, as Leo the Great expresses it, "our desires are directed beyond the range of our sight."[6] Augustine also expresses such desire beautifully: "For we

---

[6] Leo the Great, "Sermon 2 on the Ascension," in *Sermons of Pope Saint Leo the Great*, 74.1, www.newadvent.org/fathers/360374.htm.

have been promised that we shall receive what we do not yet possess; and since he is true to his promises, we rejoice in hope; but since we have not received what he promised, we sigh in longing. It is good for us to persevere in longing, until the promise comes true and sighing is a thing of the past, and unalloyed rejoicing takes its place."[7] It is this desire and longing for Easter that motivates us to make our Lenten journey in the joy of the Holy Spirit (49.6).

The Goal of Our Lenten Journey: Easter

Of course, Easter is more than the annual celebration at the end of the Lenten journey. We await it and celebrate it at every moment. This central mystery of Christ's death and resurrection is fundamental to the whole of our lives and this reality is reflected in the Rule. The whole Rule is an Easter document, written in the light of the resurrection and calling us to a continual encounter with the risen Christ. This is so from the opening call, including the baptismal call (Prol. 14), through the path of conversion and Gospel living, to the ultimate experience of love and arriving "all together to everlasting life" (72.12). Therefore, there is no one chapter that sums up how Benedict thinks about Easter, although Easter is a pivotal principle for the way in which Benedict gives shape to the life the monks live—times, meals, structure of the days and the seasons, and prayer (10.1; 15.1; 41.1; 48.3). In order to gain some deeper insight into how central Easter is for our whole way of life, I will now examine some aspects connected with the Sacred Triduum leading up to Easter.

---

[7] Augustine, "Exposition of Psalm 148," in *Expositions of the Psalms (Enarrationes in Psalmos) 121-150 III/20*, trans. Maria Boulding, The Works of Saint Augustine, a Translation for the 21st Century, vol. 6 (Hyde Park, NY: New City Press, 2004), 479.

Holy Thursday

As we celebrate Holy Thursday in the liturgy, there are some striking elements that can remind us of important areas in the Rule. It is almost impossible to participate in this celebration and not think of these. This is not surprising given the strong connection of the Rule with Scripture, liturgy, and life. We first have Benedict's understanding of the place of the table and the meals in our cenobitic living. Then we have the great symbol of the washing of the feet. And also we hear from Jesus himself the crucial declaration, "This is my Body given for you." Often the way we give ourselves to others in our community living and the way we wash each other's feet is symbolized by our gathering at the table. As Jesus in his lifetime made this ultimate gift of himself, the call for us to do likewise is a call to very radical discipleship following in Jesus' steps. A very general reference to some of the texts involved will illustrate the view that Benedict's Rule presents a paschal manner of life.

Service and love are linked in chapter 35, "On the Weekly Kitchen Servers" (35.1, 6). Such things as the care of the weak (35.2-3), the consideration for those with other duties (35.5, 12), and the concern and reverence shown in the prescription about cleaning, washing the towels and utensils, and the washing of the feet (35.7-10), all reflect the significance for Benedict of loving service, and also of how central for him is the common table in the lives of monks. The exclusion chapters, which indicate that certain monks are to be banished for their faults from the table as well as the oratory, again show this (24–25). Likewise, we note that part of their satisfaction and reconciliation process is a return to the common table (43–44). Benedict also sees fit to devote two whole chapters to details of food and drink, thus showing the significance of meals and table in the community life (39–40).

Central to chapter 35 is the washing of the feet. We can easily see how important this action is as a symbol of service when we read that guests have their feet washed by the abbot (53.12). The action as described in the Rule must surely remind us of the gospel passage read on Holy Thursday, in which we see Jesus' action as one of service and love (John 13). Thus, our bearing toward one another must arise out of our life in Christ Jesus (Phil 2:6). The words of the Last Supper, "This is my Body given for you," are given a practical expression in this highly symbolic gesture. Indeed, "there is no greater love than this, to lay down one's life for one's friends" (John 15:13). Thus we have the gospel text enacted in liturgy and lived out in life.

Good Friday

On Good Friday the cross stands clearly and starkly as the central symbol. The cross, the tree of life, is at the center of the Christian life and, hence, of the way of life Benedict presented. Here we see the paschal mystery in all its fullness. As Christ's death led to the glory of the resurrection and all that this risen life implied, so the road that the Rule describes, though narrow, leads to life (Prol. 48; Matt 7:14). The depth of the text that Benedict quotes as a central text on obedience, "I did not come to do my own will, but the will of the one who sent me" (John 6:38), leads us into the mystery of the cross (5.13). So, too, does the end of the Prologue: "We will participate in the Passion of Christ through patience so as to deserve to be companions in his kingdom" (Prol. 50). There is a close connection here with the Pauline text, "He humbled himself and became obedient to the point of death—even death on a cross" (Phil 2:8). This is the same attitude with which one must embrace even hostile or unjust things patiently, with no outcry (7.35). There is no doubt that one must deny oneself in order to follow Christ (4.10). The very reason for embracing the cross is to follow Christ who, in fact, took up his cross and hence gave us the power to do so. Like him, we too will find resurrection and eternal life through the cross.

Holy Saturday

Celebrating Holy Saturday—the day of vigil, silence, waiting, and desire—can make us remember Benedict's emphasis on these aspects of our living. There is "the great importance of silence itself," its "intrinsic value" (6.2-3), the gentleness and seriousness with which we should speak (7.60), and "the love for silence" we should have (7.56). A sense of eagerly watching and waiting is expressed in chapter 22, describing the monks' sleeping arrangements and their readiness for the Work of God in the night. This same readiness and expectancy is also described in chapter 43 on the ready response that we should make at all times to the signal for the Divine Office.

Then we move through Holy Saturday to the celebration of the great Paschal Vigil. We celebrate the memorial of our baptism, being reminded of the baptismal call and response in the Prologue (v. 14), and we experience the transforming power of the Word of God as we listen to the Vigil readings recounting God's great deeds. This seems to be an intense focusing of the monk's attentive daily listening to God's Word throughout his life.

Easter

And so the serious journey undertaken at the beginning of Lent brings us to the encounter with the risen Christ. It is a loving encounter, reflecting the risen Jesus' encounter with the apostles and Mary Magdalen. Our faith is deepened, as was that of Thomas. We walk in a new way with burning hearts, as did the disciples on the Emmaus road (John 20–21; Luke 24). In the same way we meet the risen Christ in the guests (53.7, 15), in the sick (36.1), in the abbot (2.2; 63.17), and in all our contacts with each other. This truth is illustrated in the story we read in Gregory the Great's *Dialogues*, about the monk who came to Benedict when he was in the cave, and of his having to remind him that Easter had arrived. The visiting monk's first greeting was, "Let us take some food. For today is Easter." Benedict replied, "I know that it is Easter because I have the honor of seeing you." We generally emphasize the fact that Benedict was so caught up in God that he had forgotten the great feast. But even more important, we can see in that beautiful response that the encounter itself was Easter for Benedict.[8] So we see it is Easter in all our encounters every day, and it is the risen Christ we meet in each other.

No wonder we are justified in singing the great Easter Alleluia! If during Lent we have refrained from the joy of the Alleluia, we can then sing it at Easter with even greater joy and intensity, our desire intensified by the deprivation. Benedict has said, "From the holy feast of Easter until Pentecost Alleluia is always said" (15.1). The Alleluia has been locked up (RM 45.9), but now Easter breaks open the Alleluia of joy: "It is forbidden to fast from Easter to Pentecost because Easter Sunday closes the fast of sadness and opens the Alleluia of joy" (RM 28.44). Desire also has the effect of increasing our capacity.

"By delaying the fulfilment of desire God stretches [our capacity], by making us desire he expands the soul, and by this expansion he increases its capacity."[9] The journey of life and of Lent may be long, but it is a journey of hope and desire. As Augustine also says, "Let us sing Alleluia here below while we are still on the journey so that we may sing it one day above when we have reached journey's end."[10]

The longing for the banquet of eternal life is here satisfied at Easter after the Lenten journey. The already experienced—and the yet to be experienced—feast of rich food and choice wines has been provided for us, food for the journey and food still to be longed for (Isa 25:6).

---

[8] *Dialogues* 2.2.7.

[9] Augustine, *Treatise on the First Letter of St John*, Homily 4.6, http://www.newadvent.org/fathers/170204.htm.

[10] Augustine, *Sermo* 256, I (PL 38, 1191).

10

"Seek Peace and Pursue It"

THE QUESTION OF RECONCILIATION IS an issue that has enormous implications for community living. What are the things that cause the need for it? How do we go about seeking peace and pursuing it? What are some of the processes that might help us to do this?

My starting point is the following "instrument of good works" in chapter 4 of the Rule: "If you have a quarrel with someone, make peace before sundown" (4.73). The source for this text is the well-known passage from Ephesians 4:26: "Be angry but do not sin; do not let the sun go down on your anger, and do not make room for the devil." The *New English Bible* translation has an interesting nuance: "If you are angry, do not let anger lead you into sin; do not let sunset find you still nursing it; leave no loophole for the devil." So the issue at hand is not the anger itself, but what we do with it. We are not to "nurse it," nor let it lead us into sin, and we are to make an effort to restore the peace. The timing "before the setting of the sun" is probably symbolic rather than always possible in practice, but it does indicate that something must be urgently done before too much time elapses.

André Louf once wrote that Christian community is built on human weakness and is therefore a place of pardon, a place of healing.[1] Most of us would surely know the weaknesses that we experience in the community; but do we always know and experience the community as a place of pardon and healing? We may well ask whether "making peace before the setting of the sun," as required by Rule (4.73), is a realistic proposal. It certainly would appear not so in the world situation at large, where the archaic eye-for-an-eye mentality seems to be the prevailing basis for actions.

When one looks at the text of the Rule overall, it would appear that Benedict of Nursia was certainly a realist. To take only some of the issues he warns against in chapter 4, we can see that he knows such things will happen, even in the best of circles. And he had probably seen them happening firsthand. Some of the points he mentions in chapter 4 point to the universality of sin—the kind of sin that corrodes the community, destroys the peace, and shows that we need to work toward wholeness and reconciliation. These corroding factors include: anger, vengeance, deceit, making false peace, returning evil for evil, murmuring, contention, envy, jealousy, hatred, and speaking ill of others. What Benedict is emphasizing is the fact that such vices and abuses should not be part of a community that is trying to live out the teaching of the Gospel. We have, however, all experienced that at least some of these faults do emerge at times in our own community lives. But if sin is rife, what about reconciliation?

1. The Corrosion of Community

It is possible to believe that the meaning of our lives is to be found in the quality of our personal relationships. We are all part of the same humanity. We learn the most valuable lessons from each other. And I think Benedict would in general agree

---

[1] André Louf, "Living in Community," *Cistercian Studies Quarterly* 21 (1986): 87.

with this. If that is so, we need to look at what damages the quality of our personal relationships and to see if we can do anything about it. I will begin by commenting on some of the points Benedict raises in chapter 4.

Anger: Apart from the text from Ephesians there is, of course, the Gospel teaching on doing something about anger. The text in Matthew, from the Sermon on the Mount, makes it very clear. Not only will murder make you liable to judgment, Jesus says, but also, "I say to you that if you are angry with a brother or sister you will be liable to judgment" (Matt 5:22). And if you express this anger by offering insult or calling a brother or sister a fool, you will be liable to the council or even to hell fire. There then follows the familiar text stating that our offerings at the altar are unacceptable unless we are previously reconciled with our brother. Only then can we "come and offer [our] gift" (Matt 5:24). So it is not the anger in itself but its expression in aggressive behavior that is the problem. Our actions are to be shaped by reason as well as by emotion. It is interesting that this instrument of good works, "You are not to act in anger," follows immediately after "Prefer nothing to the love of Christ" (4:21). Clearly this implies that it is the love of Christ that should shape how we conduct our lives, and that this same love makes it possible to disarm anger. For lovers of Christ there is no room for malice, no room for the vicious circle of evil in which injustice begets injustice and violence begets violence. Only love can break this cycle. Someone must absorb the violence and refuse retaliation.

The *desire for vengeance* is connected to the passion of anger. Dysinger translates this tool (4.23) as "not to store up wrath, awaiting a time of revenge."[2] Here what is manifested is a sort of smoldering resentment which, if allowed to grow, will eventually be expressed in aggression.

---

[2] Luke Dysinger, trans., *The Rule of Saint Benedict: Latin & English* (Trubuco Canyon, CA: Source Books, 1997).

Deceit and *false peace* (4.24-25) both indicate a lack of honesty. The appearance may exist that all is well, but internally resentment is flourishing. Jeremiah puts it well: "They all speak friendly words to their neighbors, but inwardly they are planning to lay an ambush" (Jer 9:8).

Returning evil for evil speaks for itself (4.29). This is the outcome of being unable to accept a wrong without retaliation. The fourth degree of humility is wholly absent from such behavior. I will come back to this point when I speak of forgiveness.

Holzherr notes that *murmuring* is a kind of fault-finding peevishness.[3] It is an insidious and destructive force in any community, and Benedict condemns it throughout the Rule in the strongest possible terms.

The Rule also lists the taking away of another's reputation, hatred, jealousy, and envy (4.40, 65-68), which are all destructive of relationships and of the trust we can have placed in one another. Contention implies habitual quarrelling and is an attitude that can grow if unchecked. Like anger, this does not have to be the outcome of conflict. It can be controlled.

Other possible faults are listed throughout the Rule, but I will not comment on them except to note them. There are those at the beginning of chapters 23 and 46, and also the terrible vice of private ownership (33). Benedict knows as well that the thorns of contention will surely spring up (13.12). He also feels the need to decry the action of one brother striking another (70.1), which he must have seen happening in his day. We know from experience that some of these things, and perhaps other faults as well, occur now as well.

In a talk he gave in 2003, Rowan Williams used a term which I find both challenging and useful. He asked the question, "What is the currency of the community?"[4] That question

[3] George Holzherr, *The Rule of Benedict: Guide to Christian Living* (Dublin: Four Courts Press, 1994), 68.

[4] Rowan Williams, "God's Workshop," talk given at Trinity Church, London, May 24, 2003.

is worth asking of ourselves and of the community. Is the accepted "currency" of our communities murmuring, or contentiousness, or judging others, or blaming others, or gossip, or lack of forgiveness? Or is it love of one another, the striving for peace, generosity, and mutual acceptance?

2. Community and Tools

In the Prologue, when Benedict uses the image of the school, he speaks of the need to rectify faults and safeguard love. Then in chapter 4 he speaks of tools and a workshop in which to work at such rectification and safeguarding. In his Trinity Church talk, Rowan Williams quotes a lovely image of tools being, for seasoned workers, like an extension of their hands, almost a part of their persons. One could also use the image of a musician and his or her instrument. The cellist Stephen Isserlis is someone who reminds me of this, as in fact do all veteran musicians. At the moment of playing, they simply become one with their instruments. Tools and instruments are worn smooth by long use. The lesson I draw from this is that it takes a very long time to work at these behavioral issues in community, in fact a lifetime. The end of chapter 4 emphasizes this when it speaks of the need for stability in the community while we work at these things. The tools have to become part of us. Cenobitic life is all about being bound up with others, about trying to develop a way we can live together stably, knowing that we will often have to practice the daily discipline of mending. This is why the focus of chapter 4 is so real: it does not envision any kind of magic or "quick fix."

3. The Processes of Reconciliation and Healing

Benedict does not merely give us directions about what to do and to what to avoid. He also gives us wise advice about what to do when relationships break down. I believe there is much to be gained from a study of chapters 23–30, which I call the corrective code, and chapters 44–46. These chapters are often neglected as irrelevant, and certainly some of the teaching therein could be regarded this way. But as usual with the Rule, if we look at the principles that Benedict is presenting, there is much to be gained. So one of the issues raised after looking at the sinfulness that can appear in the community is how we go about reconciliation. There is little difficulty in recognizing the faults that are part of the human condition, but it is not so easy to remedy the situation when these faults occur. I want to make some points about the teaching contained in these chapters.

a) Faults Do Not Go Unchecked

The first point that should be obvious from these chapters is that in Benedict's view, faults are not to go unchecked. Warnings are given, first in private. Then, if there is no amendment, there is public rebuke. As a last resort the erring one is excommunicated. This means that the person is cut off from the community— no contact is allowed (25.2; 26.1-2)—and, depending on the gravity of the fault, he or she cannot participate in community meals or prayer. This is a great deprivation for those who love the community. It seems to me, however, that Benedict intends the punishment to be a stimulus to making satisfaction and amending the wrong behavior, because the isolation enables the person to face the truth honestly (25.3). Misguided sympathy and contact can prevent this. All of it is supposed to bring about healing, as underscored by the final words of this set of chapters: *ut sanentur*—"that they may be healed" (30.3). Those who do not amend must finally undergo the terrible process of being completely and definitively cut off from the community, a series of steps graphically described in chapter 28.

b) But All Is Done with Compassion

The seeming harshness of the punishment, however, is very much mitigated by the compassion that Benedict at the same time enjoins, and this is my second point. He always speaks of the excluded one as a "brother," albeit one who at times behaves like a delinquent; or he is viewed simply as a wavering, weak, or sick brother (27.1, 3, 6; 28.5). In chapter 27, which in my opinion is one of the most beautiful chapters in the Rule, Benedict shows great compassion. The abbot who has imposed the punishment, acting as a wise physician, sends in older and wiser brothers to console the excommunicated brother and urge him to make satisfaction, "thus comforting him, lest he be devoured by excessive sorrow" (27.3). "Let love for him be intensified," Benedict says. All of this is to be done out of caring with all solicitude for those who have erred.

c) Reconciliation and Healing Can Be Slow and Painful

The third point that I think emerges from these chapters is that Benedict understands that healing and reconciliation can be a rather slow process. The provisions he makes indicate this. Time is to be made for pondering, isolation, and the gradual nature of the reintegration into the community. Healing can not only be slow but also very painful as one experiences growth in self-understanding, is able to admit the fault, grows in understanding of the need to change, and begins to undertake whatever means are necessary for this. Here real humility is called for, knowing our own weakness and knowing that we must depend on God only. In a radio program some time ago, a Tasmanian sculptor was interviewed who had designed a garden of reconciliation. He described the huge rock that is the main feature of this garden. This rock is split down the middle, and the sculptor commented that you must let the world break your heart before you can forgive and be truly reconciled.

d) Rituals Play a Very Important Part

Another thing Benedict so clearly understood about the process of healing is the vital place that rituals occupy. He had already stated this when he noted in chapter 13, "On the Recital of the Lord's Prayer," that at the end of Lauds and Vespers, the

thorns of scandal are likely to spring up (13.12). And toward
the end of the Rule he describes another very important ritual:
if a brother is rebuked by a senior, he should immediately and
without delay cast himself on the ground at his feet, remaining
there to do penance until the turmoil is healed by the other's
blessing (71.8).

In our present context of reconciliation after faults, the most
significant use of ritual is the gradual reacceptance of the erring member back into the community, as described in chapter
44. This chapter describes the person lying face down on the
ground at the feet of all as the monks leave the oratory. Then,
when the abbot decides, the erring monk prostrates himself
at the abbot's feet and then at the feet of all so that they may
pray for him. Then he may be received back into the oratory,
but not necessarily in his former rank. He cannot lead a psalm
or a reading, and at the end of each hour of the Work of God
he is to prostrate himself in the place where he stands. Finally,
when he has made satisfaction, he can resume his place in the
community. Though we no longer use such rituals, we could
nevertheless ask what rituals, if any, we do presently have,
for example when someone distances himself or herself from
the community? What rituals, if any, do we have for healing,
for forgiveness, and for reconciliation?

4. Forgiveness and Reconciliation

This is not the place to attempt to solve the problems caused
by sinfulness in our communities. But it is very relevant to
ask ourselves just how it is that we go about forgiveness and
reconciliation in the concrete. Benedict's teaching on the processes we have just discussed are important; but perhaps there
is still room for expansion.

Let us first look at forgiveness. I do not believe that reconciliation can happen in the absence of forgiveness. The need
for forgiveness is plain Gospel teaching: "How often must I
forgive?" asked Peter. "Seven times?"—"I say to you," Jesus

answered, "seventy-seven times" (Matt 18:22), which means over and over and over again.

The word "forgiveness" means letting go of hatred, refusal to maintain the need for revenge, going beyond what is expected. There is a perfect example of this in an article Sheila Cassidy wrote in *The Tablet* some time ago. After a very difficult circumstance in her life and after very painful reflection, she came to say:

> However much we have been wronged, however justified our hatred, if we cherish it, it will poison us. Our hearts will become bitter and our vision clouded and our love will wither away. Hatred is a devil to be cast out and we must pray for the power to forgive, for it is in forgiving our enemies that we are healed. Hate is always tragic. It distorts the personality and scars the soul. It is more injurious of the hater than it is of the hated.[5]

We could think of many examples where hatred is put aside in the process of working to forgive. Think of the case of Cardinal Bernardin and his accuser. Think of the Trappist monk Fr. Christian de Chergé, who in anticipation called his murderer-to-be "the friend of his final moment" and who commended this murderer "to the God whose face I see in yours." In the Genesis story of Joseph (Gen 42–47), we note the memorable statement that Joseph made when he finally told his brothers who he was: "Come closer to me. . . . I am your brother Joseph, whom you sold into Egypt. And now do not be distressed or angry with yourselves, because you sold me here; for God sent me before you to preserve life" (Gen 45:4-5). Here is complete forgiveness, showing the outcome of reflecting on the meaning of the tragic event, an event that should not have happened and that could have engendered great hatred and

---

[5] Sheila Cassidy, "Seventy Times Seven," *The Tablet* (March 2, 1991): 268.

the need for revenge. It is not hard to think of examples. But it is harder to put this truth into practice in our own lives. Perhaps the first act toward forgiveness is to acknowledge one's own sin. If we do this, then we can more easily take the second step, namely, forgetting wrongs and controlling temper. Then forgiveness can happen. Knowing our own sinfulness makes it easier to forgive the sinfulness of others.

We need to remember that forgiveness is indeed an act of love. Perhaps the real issue here is that we do not have enough love. If we can forgive, we can then make the move to reconciliation. This word implies a move back to union—it is a seeking of wholeness.

Benedict is emphatic about the abbot's role in the reconciliation process. Three things stand out in connection with this, and they apply not only to the abbot but also to all of us. These are compassion, service, and accountability. Every effort toward forgiveness and reconciliation must involve compassion. The struggle to maintain this attitude in an endeavor to bring about reconciliation requires a willingness to serve, both for the good of the person and for that of the community. Then there is the fact that the abbot is accountable for those in his care. These three things are aspects of our mutual love for one another, and are therefore the responsibility of us all; but perhaps the abbot is in a privileged position to ensure that what circulates in the community is an effort toward reconciliation, forgiveness, nonjudgmentalism, and peacemaking. Thomas Aquinas has a striking formulation in his commentary on the Gospel of Saint John. Speaking of shepherds, he says: "No one can be a good shepherd unless he is united with Christ through charity. . . . Two things are required of him, to be responsible for [the sheep] and to love them; one is not enough without the other."[6]

---

[6] Thomas Aquinas, *Commentary on John's Gospel* 10.3 (Office of Readings, Monday, Twenty-First Week of Ordinary Time).

5. God's Forgiveness

I would like to conclude this chapter with a reminder of the power of God's forgiveness. At bottom we must forgive because, like God, we cannot find it in our hearts to do otherwise. This goes to the heart of the matter. Note that the instruments of good works which precede and follow the one we began with—"If you have a quarrel with someone make peace before sundown" (4.73)—really sum up all we have been considering. The preceding instrument is: "Pray for your enemies for the love of Christ" (4.72). Just as at the end of chapter 7, where Benedict changes the text of the Master in order to give full centrality to Christ, so too here he sees that forgiveness is only possible if Christ helps to make it so. And then follows the final instrument, with which he ends chapter 4 overflowing with hope despite the difficulty of all of this. He enjoins: "And never despair of God's mercy" (4.74).

Indeed, these are the things that make it possible for us to live together as a community and that also make the Christian community's ways to be different from the ways of the world.

11

Obedience

A Listening Stance

WE CAN APPRECIATE SOMETHING OF the importance of obedience in Benedict's mind in several ways. It is a very significant part of the "spiritual" chapters (chaps. 1–7). He introduces it at the very beginning of the Rule: "The labor of obedience will bring you back to him from whom you had drifted through the sloth of disobedience" (Prol. 2). There are also chapters specifically on obedience and mutual obedience (chaps. 5, 68, and 71), and Steps 2–5 in chapter 7, "On Humility," also relate to it. The words *oboedientia* and *oboedire* are used about 35 times throughout the Rule.

We can think about obedience by examining it from the following points of view:

- Obedience to God's Word
- Obedience to the Rule
- Obedience to one another
- Obedience to the abbot

Obedience: A Willing and Eager Response

Terrence Kardong's translation of the Rule describes obedience in this way: "Obedience must be acceptable to God and humanly attractive" (5.14). Its being humanly "attractive," however, does not lessen the difficulties that will emerge at times in connection with obedience. The following texts express something of this in the way they speak of struggle or effort:

- "Therefore we must prepare our hearts and our bodies to wage the battle of holy obedience to his precepts" (Prol. 40).
- "Returning by the labor of obedience to the one from whom you drifted through the inertia of disobedience . . . , renouncing self-will . . . , take up the powerful and shining weapons of obedience to fight for the Lord Christ, the true King" (Prol. 2-3).
- "We are to have nothing whatsoever of our own. . . . That is because they have neither their bodies not their own wills at their own disposal" (33.4).
- After profession, the person is considered a member of the community, so possessions are to be given away, nothing is to be kept back for self, "since he knows that from henceforward he does not even have any more power over his own body" (58.25).
- "They should bear each other's weaknesses of both body and character with the utmost patience" (72.5).

The Scripture texts cited in chapter 5 are very important because they emphasize the immediacy of the response needed. There is difficulty at times; there must be an attitude of listening; and then the response at times requires the forsaking of one's own will. This leaves us in no doubt about what is expected. We are expected to be not only willing but also even eager. These themes are evident in the following texts:

No sooner did he hear than he obeyed me (Ps 18:45; RB 5.5).

Whoever listens to you, listens to me (Luke 10:16; RB 5.6, 15).

Narrow is the road that leads to life (Matt 7:14; RB 5.10).

I have come to do not my own will, but the will of him who sent me (John 6:38; RB 5.13).

Obedience to God's Word

Basic to all of this, and a requirement that will enable us to hear what God is saying and then respond, is our listening to God's Word throughout our lives. If we are to be obedient to God's Word we are called: to be a listener, to be a disciple, to discern, to discover God's will, to be faithful, and to be transformed. Let us now examine each of these effects of obedience.

a) To Be a Listener

If we are to listen, we must get to the very heart of our being. As when we listen to each other, listening to the Word of God takes effort, concentration, and attention. God's Word is alive and active; it cuts through like a double-edged sword (Heb 4:12). We listen with our ears and with our hearts. In chapter 5 we note the interiority envisioned in verses 17-18: "If we murmur not only with our lips but even in our hearts, then, even if we obey, it is not acceptable to God who sees the heart of the murmurer." The Word is ever asking to enter our hearts, and we must give our consent and respond.

Sr. Aquinata Böckmann speaks of the use of intensive language and negative language in chapter 5. This usage tells us something of the urgency of the subject and the willingness that is required in our responses. She notes that intensives are used mainly in the first part: "without delay" (1-4); "at once"; "with the quick feet of obedience" (8); "at the same moment"; "speedily"; "in swiftness" (9); "to hold nothing dearer than Christ" (2).

Negatives, which indicate a slow or unwilling response, are used mainly in the third part: "without hesitation, slowness, lukewarmness, grumbling, or an unwilling reply" (14); the warning against ill will and murmuring in the heart (17); the punishment due to murmurers (19).[1]

---

[1] A. Böckmann, "RB 5: Benedict's Chapter on Obedience," *American Benedictine Review* 45, no. 2 (June 1994): 112.

b) To Be a Disciple

We hear the call and try to respond, to follow. It is the total person who responds with ears, hands, feet, mouth, desires, mind, and heart. We can be a cheerful follower or an unwilling one. Being the former is a sign of a free and integrated person.

Sometimes the Word will call us to suffering—as it did Christ himself—as for example in the fourth degree of humility. Here we are reminded that our efforts may be surrounded by difficult, unfavorable, or even unjust conditions. If this happens, we must embrace the suffering and not seek to escape it (7.35-36). Part of being a follower of Christ is the willingness to take up the cross daily (cf. Mark 8.34). We can choose to respond to this Christ whom we follow, the one who calls us in so many ways, because, as the opening of chapter 5 says, "we esteem nothing as more beloved than Christ"; "we hold Christ more precious than anything"; and "we cherish Christ above all"—as the different translations have it.

Discipleship also is connected to the ideas of listening, of gradually learning, of following, and to the inherent idea of discipline.

c) To Discern

It is at this level of listening to God's Word in Scripture that discernment takes place. We are reminded of the primacy of silence, solitude, *lectio*, prayer, and stability if we are to live a life of discernment. This demands asceticism. Perhaps we too often equate discernment with decision making. We can never truly discern, individually or communally, if we are not all along living lives that are open to God's Word.

d) To Discover God's Will

Discovering God's will is related to our ability to listen. We must hear God's Word as it is really calling us, and not just use this Word to confirm us in following our own desires. Real asceticism is required here.

This is the narrow way. We must be open enough to admit that not every desire of our heart is good or God inspired. If we are not challenged by and open to God's Word, it is very easy to become a sarabaite: "Their law consists in their own willful desires: whatever they think fit or choose to do, that they call holy; and what they dislike they regard as unlawful" (1.8-9). We cannot just "follow our dream" instinctively unless to this dream we bring a real openness to the truth. God's Word as spoken through the Rule, the superior, and our sisters and brothers can also prevent us losing sight of this pursuit of truth. To be open to this, I believe that the first step must be our relationship to God's Word in our daily *lectio* and liturgy.

"I did not come to do my own will but the will of him that sent me" (John 6:38) is a crucial text in chapter 5 (v. 12). Following Christ in this manner is part of the narrow way. Benedict uses this text after a section of chapter 5 where he uses very dynamic active participles, as Sr. Aquinata Böckmann points out: *living*—not according to our own estimation; *obeying*—not our own desires and pleasures; *walking*—by another's judgment; and *dwelling*—in communities. She notes that "living" and "obeying" speak of an interior attitude, while "walking" and "dwelling" make this concrete. In this way we know and learn to do God's will.[2]

e) To Be Faithful

Let us note how interconnected all these points are. Openness comes as we daily listen. Our practices are where our ascetical effort is realized in the concrete. Being faithful requires that we put other things aside, that we make time, that we be able to give our best selves to this endeavor, or—if we simply can't, if we are too tired—that we just "be there" and wait on God. But we need always to make the space necessary within ourselves and our lives, as is suggested in chapter 48, the space where

---

[2] Böckmann, "RB 5," 119.

we are called to a balanced life and where we can be "empty" for God. We are called to be full of faith.

f) To Be Transformed

"To learn to know the heart of God in the words of God"[3]: this is how Gregory the Great expresses the transformation involved here. It happens gradually over a lifetime as we struggle to listen to God's Word daily, to hear and respond to the call to discipleship, to discern God's will, to put aside self, to be faithful. We become Christ, we are identified with him, we come to see with the mind and heart of Christ. In other words, *we are Christ.* And this becomes evident in our whole person, as in the twelfth degree of humility, in which a person manifests humility in his or her whole person, both externally and internally, and in whatever activity has been engaged. It is total transformation and integration (7.62-66).

Obedience to the Rule

The heading over chapter 1 of the Rule is: "Here begins the text of the Rule. It is called a rule because it regulates the lives of those who obey it." In what sense does it "regulate"? Benedict is obviously emphasizing this idea. For context we note what he says about the sarabaites: "They are the most detestable kind of monks with no rule to guide them. Their law is their own willful desires and they choose to do whatever they like" (1.6-9).

We need to have a very balanced and gentle approach to any "rule," to think of it as a plan for life, a set of principles which are moderate and adaptable. We have to make the Rule of Benedict livable; but we do need a framework, something that expresses our way of life. For Benedict it is "a little rule for beginners." It is a particular expression of the Gospel way of life. His Rule contains both principles and practical ways by which these principles are lived.

[3] Gregory the Great, *Registrum Epistolarum*, Book 4, Letter 31.

So we ask what practices it takes for us to be willing and eager to live the Benedictine way of life. Let us consider the following:

a) To Be in a School

There has to be organization for any group of people who live and work together; but Benedict says that, though perhaps the way of life he envisions will be a little strict at times, nonetheless there is to be nothing harsh or oppressive about it (Prol. 46). Being in a school includes the idea of learning, of being open, of admitting to what we don't yet know. Then there is also the idea of working with others and the consequent need for collaboration and a willingness to listen to what others have to teach.

b) To Hear Heart Speaking to Heart

Our consciousness is gradually formed by the way of life that we live, so that we can comprehend the demands of each concrete situation and respond to the Word of God as it is revealed to us through the actual life of the community. We need to develop a monastic and Benedictine heart. We hope eventually to come to love this way of life and no longer want any other.

c) To Live Within a Corporate Framework

The common rule as described in the eighth step of humility can be very demanding: "A monk does only what is endorsed by the common rule of the monastery and the example set by his superiors" (7.55). It is easy to be always able to see a theoretically better way. We have to learn when to speak and when not to speak. This does not mean, however, that we canonize the *status quo*.

Whatever Benedict intended by this eighth step, we can be reasonably sure that he did not envisage dehumanizing monasticism to the extent that the *status quo* had the only claim to moral rectitude, and that the only way to operate was always to go through the correct channels and "procedures." So often we unconsciously set up again within the monastery the worst qualities of the very world we have fled. We continue living within institutional structures run by committees and resting on a bureaucracy that can depersonalize, though admittedly some of this is at times necessary.[4] Ultimately we have to learn to accept decisions once made, and not to murmur.

Obedience to One Another

Another aspect of obedience is mutual obedience. It may be that we will not frequently confront the concrete demands of obedience to a superior and a Rule; but certainly obedience to God's Word is a daily experience, and so too is obedience to one another. Chapter 71 states the need for mutual obedience in absolutely clear terms: "Obedience is a blessing to be shown by all, not only to the abbot but also to one another as brothers, since we know that it is by this way of obedience that we go to God" (71.1-2).

This means being mutually dependent on one another in our seeking of God, holding all things in common, bearing one another's burdens, and supporting and encouraging one another. In this way we experience and express in community the love of Christ.

We can spell out some of the concrete ways by which we live this out under the following headings.

We Need . . .

. . . to be free and responsible

Sometimes it can seem that freedom and responsibility are opposed to one another. How can we be both free and yet

---

[4] Michael Casey, *Truthful Living: Saint Benedict's Teaching on Humility* (Petersham, MA: St. Bede's Publications, 1999), 200.

also responsible? This is a crucial issue, one that requires great maturity and a real and deep understanding of what freedom means. It also raises the question of accountability, which is a very significant matter in chapter 3 of the Rule. The abbot must carefully listen to the community before making a decision, but the community likewise must express its opinions in a suitable way and so accept coresponsibility for the decision that is finally made.

Benedict expects us to show great solicitude and even anxious care for the excommunicated, the sick, and the guests. Surely that same care should be shown to one another all the time. This is difficult and demanding. The climate of individualism, of self-development, and of the satisfaction of needs or wants absorbed from our society makes difficult at times the self-forgetfulness required for mutual care and solicitude. We are all responsible for each other, for the common purse, and for our house and all its goods. The Rule of the Master expresses it thus: "Everything belongs to everyone and to no one" (RM 16.61). This is not as it sounds on first hearing: we know what happens to what belongs to no one! It means we are all responsible, but we cannot possess things as if they belong to us personally. There needs to be a healthy concern for the other so that we don't live in boxes and thus accept no responsibility for anything or anyone.

. . . to find real life in the present situation

We are called to stay with the circumstances in which we find ourselves, though Benedict does have a process for dealing with situations that are impossible (68). This is what stability calls us to. The culture of the times makes this difficult. It is easy to seek change or escape. Benedict says that we should not try to escape, even from suffering (fourth degree of humility). We have pledged our very selves to one another and to this place and to these circumstances. For the most part it is here we will find who we are in ourselves and who we are before God within the process of doing the ordinary things of daily life. This is what sustains us on our spiritual journey.

. . . to bear the weaknesses of others

We do not need to be told that others have weaknesses that must be borne. We know it by experience. The opening of chapter 23 shows that Benedict expected that the community would include the defiant, the disobedient, the arrogant, murmurers, those who want to own everything, the lazy, the ambitious, etc. Why are we, then, so surprised when we come across something less than perfection in ourselves and others? It does take great maturity to live with the daily aggravations of our lives, not to mention major personality problems and conflicts.

It seems to me that Benedict wants us to be especially concerned for the poor of whatever kind, the sick who complain, people who ask for things at the wrong time, those who would defend others. Never must we frighten the weak away. We are not to judge, for the simple reason that we know our own weaknesses and are therefore not entitled to judge others harshly. We can connect with others by our own willingness to recognize our own faults and hence understand God's mercy.

. . . to serve

To serve one another is an expression of our mutuality and our obedience to one another. For Benedict the central symbol for such mutuality is the washing of the feet in imitation of Christ washing his apostles' feet (see chaps. 35 and 53; cf. John 13:3-16). The questions of Basil the Great, "Whose feet will you wash? Whom will you serve?" find an echo in Benedict's injunction, *Serve one another in love* (35.6). We serve one another at table; guests and the sick are served in appropriate ways; service is expressed in the attitudes of the cellarer and the porter. All of this requires that we absolutely put others ahead of ourselves and that we show real obedience to others. Practiced on a daily basis, this manner of living can be extraordinarily challenging because it demands that we move beyond our own desires.

Obedience to the Abbot

Our commitment is not only to constant listening and responding to the Word of God, to living faithfully under a Rule, and to mutual relationships in the community. We are also committed to obedience to the abbot. Tomes have been written on the role of the abbot, but here we will only highlight a few pertinent points.

Benedict speaks of "serving under a rule and an abbot": *militans sub regula vel abbate* (1.1). The word *sub* ("under"), when used with *militans* ("soldiering"), gives the sense of a particular group with a special purpose, an *esprit de corps*. The word can connote "under the shelter of," "near to," "close to" (as in the case of soldiers near a standard), "under the influence of," or "under the effect of something or someone." So there is in this little word *sub* much more than just the sense of "beneath" or "subject to."

The nature of the interaction of community, Rule, and superior is a dynamic one. We note how often Benedict reminds us that the abbot is also subject to the Rule (2.4, 12-13; 64.7, 20). Benedict also reminds us that we had a choice about living within this framework (5.12). In fact, we had a choice about whether we desired to live this way of obedience: "This is the law under which you are choosing to serve. If you can keep it, come in. If not, feel free to leave." (58.10).

One of the chief aspects of the role of the abbot stated in chapter 2 is that the abbot is believed to hold the place of Christ in the monastery (2.2). Thus, Benedict notes that this person, elected to lead the community to Christ, must be both a leader and a teacher. He must make Christ known in the community by both his teaching and his example (2.11-14). He must strive to unite the community in Christ.

In Benedict's mind, the abbot is the ultimate authority; but, as chapter 3 reminds us, he must listen to the community, and only after deep reflection on what he has heard should he make the final decision. It is at this point that obedience to the abbot is exercised in the acceptance of such a decision.

Chapter 2 is entitled "On the Qualities of the Abbot." Such qualities as knowing how to exercise responsibility for the community, showing equal love for all, knowing how to deal with different personalities, and accommodating each one's character are described throughout the chapter. Likewise in chapter 64, the idea of accountability is again stressed, and then Benedict describes the love that the abbot is to show to the brothers, the moderation that he should exercise as leader, and the example he should give. Chapter 27 adds another dimension to all of this by describing the absolute care that the abbot is to show for the straying. The images of the Good Shepherd and the physician drive home the point with great force.

Chapter 5 calls for unhesitating obedience, an obedience based on love for Christ. We must strive to make a spirit of ready obedience evident in our listening and responding to God's Word, to the requirements of the Rule, to one another, and to the person elected to lead the community. If we are sincere in our efforts to do this, we will indeed be a community living our way of life with the Gospel for our guide.

12

Listening with the Heart

WE ALL KNOW THAT THE "ART" or "skill" of listening is fundamental if we are to live authentic lives. We need to be able to listen to ourselves, to others, to God, to the world, and to the land. This is a way of being connected with all that is around us, with the most important things of our lives, as we search to attain wholeness.

The importance of listening is not just a modern realization. The opening sentence of the Rule of Benedict calls us to listen and reminds us of the need for deep listening: from the heart (Prol. 1). If we are to listen like this, however, we must first hear what is being said. Hearing presumes the capacity for silence. After this we must internalize what we have heard and respond in some way. We need to have an awareness that turns listening from an activity merely of ear and brain into a living response. We must hear and heed.

All of this Benedict knew by experience and common sense, but I am sure that many professional psychologists would say the same. We ourselves also know the importance of listening in our daily lives, and of being listened to. So let us draw out some of these points.

Listening Is a Quality of Being a Disciple

A disciple is not just a follower. To be a disciple means being a learner, and the process of learning is lifelong. We will learn

128

if we listen to the wisdom of others—in their books, in inter-actions with them, and from their experience—and then we learn further as we reflect on our own experience.

Listening Demands Stillness of Heart

In order to listen we need a quiet inner space within ourselves so we can hear a special word spoken to us out of the midst of the multitude of sources that surrounds us. Then we must ponder what that word means. If we have stillness of heart, we will exhibit a reverent, ready, and humble way of listening.

Listening Demands that We Put Aside Self-Absorption

We have to listen to others without interrupting, without thinking of our response while they are talking, without think-ing of our own experience when they are describing theirs. We have to listen not only to the words but also to what is behind the words, what is being reflected about the other's feelings. We have to put aside our own agenda at least temporarily. We must not speak at the same time as the other is speaking, criti-cize what is being said, offer unsought advice. We need to be companionable listeners, not strategic advisers. We must not jump in to correct or defend. We have to be entirely present. We need patience, tolerance, good humor, and generosity. We can learn that our own needs can sometimes wait.

Listening Demands Silence

Silence is at the heart of listening; afterward, when we do speak, our words will come out of a rich soil. This is because silence is a contemplative thing. In the silence, our life of prayer can grow. We hear God only in silence. Silence helps us to weigh our words. As we grow in an interior life, the things that are sinful and negative recede within us: for in-stance, brashness, overassertiveness, hypercriticism, backstab-bing, viciousness, sarcasm, malice. In their place there begin to grow in us interior serenity, calmness, gentleness, wisdom.

Our vision becomes simpler. We are learning what is of God and what is not of God. We will also find that the need for silence grows. We do not have to fill every possible space with a deluge of words.

We also need to look at silence as being much more than a mere absence of speech. Silence also includes absence of noise, noise that distracts our attention and takes away our concentration. There also needs to be an absence of disturbance. Intrusive noise batters us and makes physical quiet more difficult. What we hear can upset us, excite us, and affect our emotions. We need to be able to sit still, to experience absence of movement. Noise often renders stillness impossible. And then we also need absence of restlessness. Restlessness is due to interior division and an inconsistency between our ideals and the reality we live.

We can learn this art of deep listening, of listening with the ear of the heart, and we need to do so if our relationships are to grow stronger. But more than an art or a skill is involved here.

All that has been said above is relevant to our prayer life, because for deep prayer the heart must have some measure of quietness. We will hear God's voice when we are silent and listen, and our lives will be gradually changed. As is often noted, the very first word of Benedict's Rule is *Listen!* And the last word in the Rule is *pervenies*, "you will arrive" (73.9). So we see that Benedict's message about life, the way of life he presents in the Rule, may be summed up in the sentence "Listen and you will arrive!" We can easily apply this to our own lives.

Listening to God

There are many ways we hear God in our lives—through our experience, through others, through nature. One of the most important ways we hear God, however, is in his very own Word, that is, in Scripture. If we read the Scriptures carefully we are led to prayer, and we must always remember that prayer is God's work. But we do have to make ourselves open and available in order to hear what God is saying. Prayer is an expression of a relationship and, as in all relationships, it is necessary to make time for the relationship to develop. As we come to this time of prayer, we pick up the book, perhaps the book of the Gospels, with great reverence and expectation. Then we read under the eye of God until our heart is touched. God will speak to us in some word that strikes us. We hear this word and then we need to ponder this word or these words until we are led to respond in prayer. It is good to be able to find a special place where we might pray, to put aside our other concerns for this short time, then to pick up the Bible and begin to read. We come to this sacred time with deep faith and love and with listening hearts. We can ask God's help as we begin.

Our constant interaction with the Word of God in the gospels or in other parts of the Bible will have a transforming effect on our relationship with God and on our lives. It is like soft water wearing away stone. Our stony hearts will be softened as we listen to God's Word with the ear of our heart, and God will become more and more important in our lives.

Listening to One Another

Benedict also knew that we often hear God speaking to us through others. We must listen intently so we can hear this message. He stresses that others are different from us, that each person has individual qualities and needs that must be acknowledged (34.3-4). He makes sure that each person receives what is necessary from the goods of the house which are to be held in common (33.6). He ensures that those who have tasks to do have what is required to carry them out (35.12-13). He asks that all accept responsibility for the care of the goods and the house (32.4). All of this requires the ability to listen to others.

Listening to Others in Their Weakness, and the Readiness to Forgive

While understanding the fragility of others, Benedict nonetheless did not back away from imposing some punishment for their failures, with a view toward healing these (24.25). One of the most beautiful parts of the Rule describes how, when wrongdoers are excluded from the community because of what they have done, the abbot should send old and wise brothers to make sure the culprits are not too weighed down by the whole process (27.2). The abbot is to go out like the Good Shepherd searching for the lost brother, leaving the ninety-nine others in the mountains (27.8). Forgiveness is always to be available for all. When there are altercations, all concerned must aim for reconciliation in peace before the setting of the sun (4.73). It is easy to see how relevant this teaching is for all our own lives today. We all have to listen to others in their weakness and respond with a readiness to forgive. We also hope to experience this same readiness from others when we ourselves fail.

Listening and Responding with Respect for All

Benedict also says that all must be treated with great respect, including the sick, the elderly, and children. The old are to love the young and the young are to respect the elders (4.71-72). Enemies are to be prayed for in the love of Christ. Guests are to be received with great reverence and love because they are welcomed as Christ. In fact, Christ is to be *adored* in them (53.1, 7). Mutual listening and responding should characterize the lives of all Christians.

All of this requires that we can exercise all the elements of listening we spoke of earlier. It is obvious that, if we are to listen to others with the ear of the heart and with deep love and respect, self-centeredness must fade out. This will demand great maturity, to the end that we may listen to the needs of others and at times even put these needs above our own. We can at least learn to listen to what is behind the behavior of others and thus become less judgmental.

As we grow in this ability to listen we will find that it becomes easier to listen attentively for the voice of God in every aspect of our lives, whether in the gospels, in one another, in the environment, or in the events of the world around us. We will be loving people with hearts that are compassionate and transformed.

At an art exhibition at the Benedictine monastery of New Norcia in Western Australia some years ago, the artist Jillian Green produced a work which consisted of two words, artistically presented. These words, "listen," and "silent," are anagrams of one another, and the artist clearly noted the connection between the two words. The picture was titled "Six Letters, Two Words, One Prayer." Perhaps our prayer could be that we will learn the value of silence in our lives so that we may listen with the ear of our heart.

13

Benedictine Tradition

Timeless and Contemporary

SPIRITUAL DISCRETION, ACCORDING TO Terrence Kardong, is
the art of applying timeless principles to contemporary realities.[1] Such discretion or discernment—a sort of sifting—is
needed for any adaptation of a tradition. In this final chapter
I want to address by way of example the question of how
the centuries-old Benedictine tradition was adapted to life
in Australia in the mid-nineteenth century when John Bede
Polding, the first Catholic archbishop of Australia, established
the community of the Sisters of the Good Samaritan of the
Order of Saint Benedict.

A Case Study of Monastic Adaptation

Such adaptation is not unusual in the Benedictine tradition. In
the Rule of Benedict itself, many examples of spiritual discretion are in evidence. Benedict says that the abbot is to adapt
the life to each one's character and intelligence (2.32); he is to
use prudence and avoid extremes (64.12); he is to be discerning
and moderate in assigning tasks (64.16). The greatest example
of Benedict's willingness to adapt the life to individual needs

---

[1] Terrence Kardong, *Benedict's Rule: A Translation and Commentary*
(Collegeville, MN: Liturgical Press, 1996), 532.

and abilities is toward the end of the chapters on the Divine Office. After spending thirteen chapters setting out details for its celebration, he says: "Above all else we urge that if anyone finds this distribution of the psalms unsatisfactory, he should arrange whatever he judges better" (18.23), to which he adds the rider "provided that the full complement of one hundred and fifty psalms is by all means carefully maintained every week, and that the series begins anew each Sunday at Vigils."

So now we ask: How did Polding adapt the timeless realities of the sixth-century Rule of Benedict to his contemporary reality of mid-nineteenth-century Australia?

The Historical Setting

The Congregation of the Sisters of the Good Samaritan of the Order of Saint Benedict began its life officially on February 2, 1857. Archbishop Polding wanted religious women to work with the poor and the destitute in the relatively wild days of early Sydney, and so he set about establishing such a group.

Polding was a Benedictine monk from Downside Abbey in England. The tradition of his own English Benedictine congregation certainly influenced him, above all in his marked missionary zeal. After the dissolution of the Benedictine monasteries during the Reformation in England, Englishmen who wanted to join Benedictine communities had to go to France. Eventually there came into being a revived English Benedictine congregation that consisted of four communities. From these communities, missionaries gradually were sent back to England. This practice resulted in a strong missionary thrust; in fact, the monks of this congregation took a fourth vow to go to the "English mission."[2] Of course, we note that there had always been a close interface between "monk" and "missionary"

[2] D. Lunn, "The English Benedictines in the XIXth Century," *Tjurunga* 8 (1974): 25–26.

throughout earlier monastic centuries. We have only to think, for example, of Augustine of Canterbury, Lioba of Wessex, and Boniface of Devon, to name but a few in the early centuries of Roman and Anglo-Saxon missionary activity by monks and nuns. It was this same spirit that, also in the mid-nineteenth century, inspired the missionary venture of Abbot Boniface Wimmer and Mother Benedicta Riepp in the establishment of Benedictine communities of men and women in America.

Polding became a Benedictine monk when he entered the community that returned to England and settled at Acton Burnell from Douai in France at the time of the French Revolution. Eventually they moved to Downside. Polding entered this community in 1810. With this missionary background in the history of Douai-Downside, it was not surprising that Polding was himself fired with missionary zeal. This impulse stood him well when he was appointed bishop for Australia and was evident in all he did. He was consecrated bishop in 1834 and arrived in Australia in 1835.

Much has been written about what has been called Polding's "Benedictine dream." It seems that he did want to establish an abbey-diocese in Australia. One element of this was Saint Mary's in Sydney, the Benedictine community of men that eventually was suppressed in 1877 by Polding's successor, Archbishop Vaughan, also an English Benedictine. It had been established in 1843. Another element of Benedictine life in Australia was the women's community at Subiaco. Sisters had come to establish this community from Princethorpe and Stanbrook, well-established Benedictine communities in England. They arrived in Australia in 1848 and eventually settled at Subiaco near Parramatta. After many struggles in their early days, especially financial ones, as well as the efforts to develop suitable rules and have them approved, this group developed into the present-day flourishing cloistered Benedictine women's community at Jamberoo in New South Wales.

I mention these two communities because the way Polding organized the rules for these two groups makes an interesting comparison with what he did for his third expression of Benedictine life in Australia: the Good Samaritans. It is usual Benedictine practice for communities to have the same basic Rule in common, and then to have Constitutions that apply the one Rule to current living situations. Though some of the dissident monks of Saint Mary's were later to claim that they had no written rules, in fact Polding had developed a document which was written in the form of "declarations," or a "commentary," inserted after each chapter of the Rule of Benedict. Terence Kavenagh, a Benedictine scholar from Sydney, notes that none of the efforts at local adaptation was especially profound. He says that, in fact, the enormous amount of time and skill invested in the Saint Mary's Declarations produced nothing of lasting significance.[3] The Subiaco women's community lived the Rule of Benedict with interpretations that were not at all adapted to contemporary life in Australia. In fact, they lived according to the Princethorpe Constitutions, which had a strong seventeenth-century French flavor. As has been said, the community struggled for a long time to develop suitable Constitutions to allow them to interpret the Rule of Benedict for current situations. This community lived a fairly traditional Benedictine life, which included an enclosure, though they did have a school for some time.

What Polding wanted, however, for his new Benedictine group, the Good Samaritans, was very different. The social needs of early Sydney were great. A refuge for women, run by a Mrs. Blake, was already in operation, first in Campbell Street and later in Pitt Street. This house had been established in 1849 and was the work of the Sisters of Charity, an Irish group who had come to Australia in 1838. The refuge was called the House of the Good Shepherd. Sr. Scholastica Gibbons was in charge of

---

[3] Terence Kavenagh, "The 1855 Monastic *Declarations* of St Mary's Sydney: Adapting *RB* to Colonial Australia," *Tjurunga* 39 (1990): 126, 152.

this refuge; but in 1853 the two sisters who worked there with her died within twenty-four hours of one another. Polding then asked Sr. Scholastica to form a new group to staff the refuge, and thus began the Sisters of the Good Samaritan. They were known at first as Sisters of the Good Shepherd, but the name was later changed because of an already existing European order by that name. The first five sisters were received on February 2, 1857. This date is commemorated as the foundation day of the congregation, and Mother Scholastica, who always remained a Sister of Charity, is regarded to be, together with Archbishop Polding, its cofounder.

The Question of Adaptation

Thomas Groome, a current writer in Catholic culture and education, when discussing adaptation and interpretation, gives three criteria for testing the authenticity of the interpretative process of texts. These three criteria—continuity, consequences, and community—can be used to test whether the so-called "timeless" principles of the Rule of Benedict can be authentically adapted to contemporary realities.[4] I believe these criteria can be so used and, in fact, I would claim that the very flexibility of the Rule, with its ability to adapt, is probably the reason for its current relevance. There are as many ways of living Benedictine life as there are communities who live by it. I hope there is no one who thinks that the only way to live Benedictine life is to be cloistered and habited! History has clearly shown otherwise.

In the discussion that follows on the "rules" that Polding gave to his new community, I will give emphasis to their continuity with the Rule of Benedict, although these rules do also show the significant efforts that Polding made to adapt

---

[4] Thomas Groome, *Sharing Faith: A Comprehensive Approach to Religious Education and Pastoral Ministry* (San Francisco: HarperCollins, 1991), 223–24.

to contemporary realities. Then I will briefly refer to the consequences of such adaptation and to the acceptance of new rules by the community.

Polding was clearly aware of the fact that he was doing something very new. In retrospect it seems even more re-remarkable that he had such an insight. The rules that he had prepared for the first five sisters show the beginnings of this adaptation. They look like this in outline:

Prologue	(RB Prol.)
Ch. 1 What are the instruments of good works	(RB 4)
Ch. 2 Of the obedience of the sisters	(RB 5)
Ch. 3 On silence	(RB 6)
Ch. 4 Of humility	(RB 7)
Ch. 5 Of the sisters rising	Directory of Visitation Nuns
Ch. 6 Of the Office	Directory of Visitation Nuns
Ch. 7 In what manner the Work of God is to be performed in the day-time	(RB 16)
Ch. 8 Of the reverence of prayer	(RB 20)
Ch. 9 Of the weekly offices which are to be in the kitchen	(RB 35)
Ch. 10 Sick Sisters	(RB 36)
Ch. 11 Whether it is lawful for a sister to receive letters or presents	(RB 54)
Ch. 12 Of the general comportment of the sisters	Rules of Sisters of Charity
Ch. 13 Rules for those who visit the sick	Rules of Sisters of Charity
Ch. 14 Of the duty of the Sisters toward the superioress	Directory of Visitation Nuns
Ch. 15 Useful Documents	Directory of Visitation Nuns
Ch. 16 Of permission for small matters common to all	Directory of Visitation Nuns

We can see how carefully this schema was constructed and how dutifully the key points of the spirituality of Saint Benedict were conserved: the Prologue, listening and responding, the Gospel way of life, community, obedience, silence, humility, service, and prayer. At the same time, the chapters that refer to the daily life and work of the new group were gathered from the two other sources noted: the Rule of the Sisters of Charity and that of the Nuns of the Visitation. These were more "modern" communities that had an external "active" ministry. (As I understand it, Saint Francis de Sales meant the Visitation community to be contemplative, but not cloistered. They carried out works of mercy to a limited degree.)

Ten years later, in 1866, the Good Samaritan rules were revised and Polding requested that they be approved. At this time he spoke of the group as a new Australian Benedictine institute.[5] Again, the Benedictine basis for the group and the need for its adaptation to the times and the place were always clear. It is also clear from the writings and notes of the early sisters that they always had access to the whole Rule of Benedict and that they were very familiar with it.

The 1866 Rules consisted of an opening section in which the scope and character of the institute was clearly defined, followed by three parts:

I. *Of the Perfection of the Oblate Sisters*
II. *Of the Works of Charity of the Institute*, and
III. *Of the Internal Government of the Institute.*

Polding used various texts as sources. One of these was the Italian translation of the Rule of Benedict used by the Benedictine women of the Cassinese Congregation. From this he took nine chapters of the Rule and material from eleven other chapters that were "declarations" on the Rule. He also used

---

[5] *Rules of Polding*, Trustees of the Sisters of the Good Samaritan (Sydney: Prior Press, 1982), 80.

sections of twenty-three chapters from the Rule and Constitutions of the Sisters of Mercy. In part three of his Rules, Polding integrated material from these two sources in a very careful way. He also used the four chapters from the Visitation Directory and two chapters from the Rules of the Sisters of Charity. These were the chapters that had been in the Rules of 1857.[6]

In the letter seeking approval, referred to above, Polding states that this community "is a society of pious women who offer themselves by vow to the practice of the spiritual and temporal works of charity under the guidance of holy obedience according to the Rule of Saint Benedict." The vows were to be made according to the spirit of the Rule of Saint Benedict. Then he goes on to say that

> the structure and practices have been taken from those already approved by the Holy See and adapted by me for this new Australian institute. They have been taken principally from the Rule of St. Benedict, from Benedictine Declarations, Constitutions and Regulations already approved, and also from the Constitutions of the Sisters of Charity likewise approved by the Church.[7]

In his response, the Consultor who was called on to examine the proposal notes that the first and third parts of the rules are almost entirely taken from the Rule of Saint Benedict and from its authentic declarations. He adds, however, that considerable modifications have been demanded by the purpose of this new institute which turns toward the active life in its works, whereas that of traditional Benedictine nuns is entirely directed toward the contemplative life. I suggest that the Consultor has here introduced a false dichotomy, since every community that engages in active works of ministry finds its meaning only in its life of contemplative prayer. He would,

[6] *Rules of Polding*, 80.
[7] *Rules of Polding*, 79–80.

however, have been using the terms "active" and "contemplative" as they were understood at that time. This was, after all, the period of the establishment of so many new orders that were not enclosed in the traditional way. The Consultor also went on to say that there would be need to modify the sections on government, since Benedictine communities would normally be independent of other monasteries, whereas in this situation, "each house or establishment of the new institute must be in continual relationship and dependence on the house where the Superior General resides."[8] This is a significant adaptation and shows that Polding already envisaged communities existing in far-flung places.

The Consultor then notes that the second part, which relates to the fulfilling of the external duties of charity that were the special object of the institute, is taken to a great extent from the Rules of the Sisters of Charity. In fact, as I have said, there were also extensive sections taken from the Rules of the Sisters of Mercy and some from the Visitation Sisters, but these were not mentioned by the Consultor.

Approval of the Polding rules was not given at this time. The difficulty seems to have been the canonical status of Mother Scholastica Gibbons, that is, whether she would be superioress of the new institute for life, as Polding wanted, and whether she would remain a Sister of Charity. Final approval of the institute was not obtained until 1932.

Some revisions of the rules were made by Polding and the Consultor, but the rules that were translated by Mr. Makinson, Polding's secretary, did not reflect these changes. In fact, it was not until 1982 that the documents relating to the 1866 request for approbation were discovered in the archives of the Propaganda Fide. Included in the find was a copy of a printed text of the rules that the Good Samaritans did not know existed. This text was then reprinted. It is the official one now used.

[8] *Rules of Polding*, 82.

It is clear in all of this that due emphasis was being given to continuity with the Benedictine basis of the Rule, and that the adaptations were being made to provide for a different way of living the Benedictine Rule according to contemporary needs and the specific purpose of the new institute. For the sections in which the adaptations were being made, texts from already approved rules were used.

A particular connection with the Benedictine basis for the rule is Polding's prescriptions about the habit. It is to be the same as that of all Benedictine nuns, Polding wrote, "that is, black habit and scapular, a double veil, that is white and black for the professed and white only for the novices in the novitiate." But there was one distinctive modification here: "They will wear a simple cross on the breast as a continual reminder of the presence of God everywhere."[9] The silver cross on a blue braid was distinctive of the Good Samaritan habit until the 1980s.

The sisters' vows were to be simple vows, made according to the spirit of the Rule of Saint Benedict, that is, on the foundation of obedience—prompt, unquestioning, and cheerful. The solemn vows made by Benedictines would have precluded the possibility of carrying out the work that Polding wanted these sisters to do outside the cloister. Though the vow formula of one of the first five sisters showed that she made the vows of poverty, chastity, and obedience, the text of the rules presented for approbation shows that Polding intended to retain the traditional Benedictine vows of stability, conversion of life, and obedience. He also arranged that the sisters would recite the Little Office of Our Lady instead of the Divine Office, no doubt because of the heavy demands of the ministry; but the daily horarium showed that the sisters recited all hours of the Little Office of Our Lady.

Though not exactly taken from the Rule of Benedict, the chapters on government contain many allusions to it. Polding

[9] *Rules of Polding*, 3.

wrote here on the election of the mother superior, on what sort of a person she should be, and on those with special roles, including frequent references to the deans, whose task in the Rule of Benedict it was to assist the abbot. After Vatican II, when the sisters took up the challenge of returning to their sources, the revised Constitutions speak very explicitly of Benedictine values in language strongly resonant of the Rule of Benedict.

Thomas Groome says that, if a text is to be authentically applied, it must be in continuity with the constitutive truths and values of the whole vision of the group, and also that it must conserve the foundational trajectory of beliefs, truths, principles, and values that are essential to the original vision.[10] Indeed, the Rules for this new institute were faithful to the original vision of Benedict.

The consequences of the adaptations made by Polding are very clear in the living out of Polding's vision for the group. His vision was expressed in the rule as follows:

> This Congregation of Religious is designed for the practice of the spiritual and temporal works of charity, under the guidance of holy obedience according to the Rule of St Benedict. Therefore as directed by their superiors the Sisters are ready to teach in Schools, to visit and assist the sick in their own homes and in hospitals, to instruct ignorant persons in the faith, to conduct Orphanages, to reform the lives of penitent women and to apply themselves to every other charitable work.[11]

This language clearly expresses the message of the New Testament in a nineteenth-century mode, but there is no doubt about what Polding wanted the sisters to do. From their beginnings at the Pitt Street refuge, the sisters later moved to

---

[10] Groome, 223–40.
[11] *Rules of Polding*, 3.

the orphanage at Parramatta, then to the industrial school at Manly, and, even before the Public Instruction Act, they were very active in education. For over a century, schools were the sisters' main ministry. The refuge work, however, continued at Saint Magdalen's Retreat at Arncliffe in New South Wales, to which neglected girls or girls from the courts were referred. There was also an orphanage maintained at Narellan in New South Wales. Currently the sisters are not so often seen in schools; but the variety of ministries in which they are engaged would indeed be a fulfilment of Polding's vision. A full discussion of this variety of ministries falls outside the scope of this chapter, though it is a fascinating story in itself.

Finally, Groome notes that a community needs to confirm the validity of their contemporary interpretation if the adaptation is to be successful.[12] It is obvious from the stories of the lives of the early sisters that they threw themselves into whatever was asked of them. Throughout the history of the Good Samaritans it can be seen that this same spirit was alive and vibrant. Where this is perhaps most obvious in recent history is in the way that, despite declining numbers and ageing members, many sisters have been led to find new venues to serve the Church. Changes in the Constitutions at six yearly general chapters were generally accepted and, as mentioned before, the community responded wholeheartedly to the renewal Vatican 11 called for.

I would like to conclude by referring to the work of a scholar of the Rule of Benedict, Father Michael Casey of Tarrawarra Abbey. In *Introducing Benedict's Rule*,[13] he refers to principles of interpretation and application. These include such things as: the fact that the Rule does not impact the community regimen directly but by way of the minds and hearts of the community

[12] Groome, 237.
[13] Michael Casey and David Tomlins, *Introducing Benedict's Rule: A Program for Formation* (Sankt Ottilien, Germany: EOS Verlag, 2006), 16–21.

members; the need to appreciate historical, cultural, and linguistic characteristics; the fact that the Rule of Benedict is part of a living tradition, so that values and beliefs of previous and subsequent traditions must be appreciated; that some aspects of the Rule of Benedict may be considered inapplicable after their meaning is closely examined; that participation in the living tradition gives "family access" to the texts which give expression to the tradition; and, finally, that the Rule enhances the consciousness of modern readers by proposing an alternative perspective.

I believe that all these principles could be applied to Polding's procedure as he established his rules for the new Australian Benedictine institute. He knew that he was setting up a whole lifestyle for his new community. He was steeped in the Rule of Benedict and its tradition. He knew that some details of the Rule were not applicable in the circumstances in which he was living. He had "family access" to the Rule because he lived it. I believe that these same points are also relevant throughout the history of the Sisters of the Good Samaritan as they have applied and continue to apply the timeless principles of the Rule of Benedict and the *Rules of Polding* to contemporary realities.

14

Communio

The Church and the Benedictine School

I HERE INTEND TO EXPLORE HOW THE Church sees the Catholic school. Following that, I will consider the particular Benedictine gift of *communio* and how this can have an effect on the future of all who are committed to Catholic education in schools that are influenced by the teaching of Saint Benedict. The question, posed in terms of the future, is: How can our schools find demonstrable ways of being both Catholic and Benedictine? How can *communio,* lived both in our lives in the Church and in our schools, be a gift for the future?

I will examine these issues in four sections:

- We will first try to delve into the depth of meaning in the idea of *communio*.
- We will then examine what the Church's documents have to say about this concept of *communio* as it might be expressed in the life of our schools.
- The substance of the chapter will then be an exploration of what Benedict has to say about living in communion.
- Finally, we will look at the implications of all of this for the future.

1. The Meaning of *Communio*

The Latin word *communio* is normally used to render the Greek word *koinonia.* It is difficult to translate this word in such a way that it conveys the full richness of its Greek connotations. It means both "communion" and "community," but it also contains the notion of intimate "participation." It evokes a sense of sharing and intimacy. It can sometimes also be translated as "fellowship," "sharing," or "contribution." It expresses above all the relationship and bond that each of us has with Jesus and the relationship of unity with other faithful that this same bond produces. *Communio,* then, is a vital and genuine connection that reaches a deep level of strong intimacy. Together, we live from the divine life, as Jesus himself suggests in the image of the vine and the branches (John 15:1). The concept also implies action, such as that required to build community or work together with others.

A person who lives in this deep communion, with Jesus and with others, shares in the possession of something that is held in common. The spirit of sharing becomes tangible and expresses itself in giving and in relinquishing an attitude of getting. What is shared, received, or given becomes common ground. This makes joint participation possible; people are recognized for who they are and they come to share the common experiences of joys, fears, and tears. Those who live in this way benefit from the experience not only of being together but also of doing together. Individual pride and vanity are overridden by what is common. An intimate relationship flourishes that embraces everyone's ideas. Even when there are congenial disagreements (or even not so congenial ones!), there is always the sense everyone's ultimate purpose is to find a common unity. An effort is steadily made to overcome brokenness and divisiveness, and much energy is invested in striving toward wholeness with other members of the group, with the environment, and with God.

The kind of unity envisaged here is expressed in Scripture passages containing the very familiar image of the Body of Christ, such as the following. Think, for instance, of the famous text from 1 Corinthians, which we should try to hear as for the first time, without allowing its familiarity to blunt its impact: "Just as the body is one and has many members, and all the members of the body, though many, are one body, so it is with Christ. For in the one Spirit we were all baptized into one body—Jews or Greeks, slaves or free—and we were all made to drink of the one Spirit. . . . Now you are the body of Christ and individually members of it" (1 Cor 12:12-13, 27). Then in Romans we read: "As in one body we have many members, and not all the members have the same function, so we, who are many, are one body in Christ and individually members one of another. Just as each of us has one body with many members, and these members do not all have the same function, so in Christ we who are many form one body, and each member belongs to all the others" (Rom 12:4). And in Ephesians, with its strong emphasis on the spiritual bond: "You were called to the one hope of your calling, one Lord, one faith, one baptism, one God and Father of all, who is above all and through all and in all. There is one body and one Spirit" (Eph 4:4-6). Though the Greek word *koinonia* is not used explicitly in these particular texts, it is evident that the biblical images of the body are very much connected with the ecclesial understanding of *communio*.

It is interesting to note that when Saint Paul uses words related to *koinonia*, there normally comes into play the ideas of partnership and deep union, as well as the idea of giving and sharing the Gospel. Here are some examples of this (the emphasis on "sharing" and "communion" is mine): "I thank my God every time I remember you, constantly praying with joy in every one of my prayers for all of you because of your *sharing* in the gospel from the first day until now" (Phil 1:5). Again in Philippians: "If there is any encouragement in Christ, any consolation from love, any *sharing* in the Spirit, any compassion and sympathy, make my joy complete: be of the same mind, having the same love, being in full accord and of one mind" (Phil 2:1). Thus, this sharing in the Spirit brings about deep communion. The Second Letter to the Corinthians ends with the familiar blessing and wish for communion: "The grace of the Lord Jesus, the love of God and the *communion* of the Holy Spirit be with all of you" (2 Cor 13:13).

Paul expresses the outcome of this fellowship in such texts as these from 2 Corinthians: He speaks of the church of Macedonia as those who "gave according to their means and even beyond their means, begging us earnestly for the privilege of *sharing* in this ministry to the saints" (2 Cor 8:4); and again, "Through the testing of this ministry you glorify God by your obedience to the confession of the gospel of Christ and by the generosity of your *sharing* with them and with all others" (2 Cor 9:13).

The greatest of all signs of fellowship in community is the Eucharist: "The bread we break, is it not a *sharing (koinonia)* in the body of Christ?" (1 Cor 10:16). The bond is mystical, a God-made spiritual unity. This is grace itself at work. Laws, obligations, formulae, liturgical rites, and the customs of daily Christian living are the outgrowth and fruit of that inner divine reality. A tangible shape is here given to actions that are consonant with divine faith and right humanity.

This is why the two texts from Acts 2:42-47 and 4:32-37 are so crucial to us when trying to plumb the depths of the meaning of *koinonia*-"communion." The ideal early Christian community is thus described: "They devoted themselves to the apostles' teaching and fellowship *(koinonia)*, to the breaking of bread and the prayers." The results of such living *koinonia* are then spelled out in the second text from Acts:

> Now the whole group of those who believed were of one heart and soul, and no one claimed private ownership or any possessions, but everything they owned was held in common. With great power the apostles gave their testimony to the resurrection of the Lord Jesus, and great grace was upon them all. There was not a needy person among them, for as many as owned lands or houses sold them and brought the proceeds of what was sold. They laid it at the apostles' feet, and it was distributed to each as any had need.

We clearly see in these two texts from Acts both the reality of the deep bond of communion among believers and its concrete outcome in terms of practical charity. As Christians gathered together in deep unity, they exhibited devotion to the teaching of the apostles, practiced the breaking of the bread, said the prayers, felt oneness of heart and soul, bore witness to the resurrection of Jesus, renounced private ownership, and held all things in common, distributing necessities to the needy: "There was not a needy person among them" (Acts 4:4).

Does all of this sound like an ideal that could never be reached in any community made up of normal human beings, whether the community of the Church, the school, the family, or indeed a religious community? That may seem so; but when we put our minds and hearts together to reflect on the challenges before us, surely these texts from Acts can urge us to consider our present circumstances and encourage us to strive toward the ideal. Here we are being given a wonderful and powerful hope, as well as an assurance of the worthwhile nature of the task to which we are committed. We know that if we can have something of this unity among ourselves, we can then reach out authentically to those who are in our care.

2. Church Documents on Education

Many of the documents of the Church on Catholic education echo these sentiments we have been discussing. In our busy lives we probably do not spend much time reading and absorbing such documents. So let us now take a little time to visit them in the light of our current context.

We will find that, not surprisingly, many of the relevant documents on Catholic education are a development and an application of the principles set forth in the documents of the Second Vatican Council. One of the most well-known and frequently quoted texts in this connection is the opening of *Gaudium et Spes*, the Constitution on the Church in the Modern World:

The joys and hopes, the grief and anguish of the people of our time, especially of those who are poor or afflicted, are the joys and hopes, the grief and anguish of followers of Christ as well. Nothing that is genuinely human fails to find an echo in their hearts. For theirs is a community of people united in Christ and guided by the holy Spirit in their pilgrimage toward the Father's kingdom, bearers of a message of salvation for all of humanity. That is why they cherish a feeling of deep solidarity with the human race and its history.[1]

We are that community now, in fact, united in a deep bond with one another and reaching out to all in their joys and hopes, griefs and anguish, at all times in our service of others.

We also know well this call from the same document: "In every age, the church carries the responsibility of reading the signs of the times and of interpreting them in the light of the Gospel, if it is to carry out its task."[2] We still strive to do this. John Paul 11 was very specific as to what that call means:

To make the Church *the home and the school of communion*: that is the great challenge facing us in the millennium which we are now beginning, if we wish to be faithful to God's plan and respond to the world's deepest yearnings. But what does this mean in practice? Here too our thoughts could run immediately to the action to be undertaken, but that would not be the right impulse to follow. Before making practical plans, we need *to promote a spirituality of communion*, making it the guiding principle of education wherever individuals and Christians are formed, wherever ministers of the altar, consecrated

---

[1] Second Vatican Council, *Gaudium et Spes* (The Church in the Modern World) in *Vatican Council II: The Basic Sixteen Documents*, trans. Austin Flannery (Collegeville, MN: Liturgical Press, 2014), 1.

[2] *Gaudium et Spes*, Flannery, 4.

persons, and pastoral workers are trained, wherever families and communities are being built up.[3]

Vatican II itself issued a Decree on Christian Education, consisting of fundamental principles that would be more fully developed by postconciliar commissions and adapted to different local circumstances by episcopal conferences. The document lays claim to the Church's obligation to fulfill her mandate to announce the mystery of salvation to all, and to promote the welfare of the whole person. We read there:

> The duty of educating belongs to the Church, not merely because she must be recognized as a human society capable of educating, but especially because she has the responsibility of announcing the way of salvation to all, of communicating the life of Christ to those who believe, and, in her unfailing solicitude, of assisting all to be able to come to the fullness of this life. The Church is bound as a mother to give to these children of hers an education by which their whole life can be imbued with the spirit of Christ and at the same time do all she can to promote for all peoples the complete perfection of the human person, the good of earthly society and the building of a world that is more human.[4]

Thus is expressed the outcome and obligation of the communion which is the Church.

This same document makes very clear what it considers distinctive about the Catholic school: this is its religious dimension, which should be in evidence in the educational climate, the personal development of each student, the relationship established between culture and the Gospel, and the illumination of all knowledge with the light of faith.[5]

---

[3] John Paul II, *Novo Millennio Ineunte*, 43.
[4] Second Vatican Council, *Gravissimum Educationis* (Declaration on Christian Education), 3.
[5] GE 8.

We can find deeply inspiring texts in the various conciliar and postconciliar documents; but here I must limit myself to enumerating some titles, hoping thereby to stimulate further reading:

1. *Declaration on Christian Education* (GE, 1965)
2. *The Catholic School* (CS, 1977)
3. *Catechesi Tradendae* (CT, 1979)
4. *The Religious Dimension of Education in a Catholic School* (RD, 1988)
5. *The Catholic School on the Threshold of the Third Millenium* (TM, 1997)
6. *Lay Catholics in Schools: Witnesses to Faith* (LC, 1982)
7. *Consecrated Persons and Their Mission in Schools* (CP, 2002)

The last two documents listed contain texts that I think can apply to all who work in Catholic education, whether religious or lay persons.

Since the topic I am addressing is the gift of *communion*, I am concentrating on the way the documents stress this and, secondly, on what results from this emphasis. If we live in a community united by our life in Christ, there necessarily are certain outcomes. It seems to me that what the documents stress over and over is the need to spread the message of the kingdom (*kerygma*) as well as the human persons involved and their development, with inclusiveness for all. Nor do these documents ignore the challenges Christians must face in attempting such a mission. Some of these challenges are: a crisis of values; the extreme pluralism that pervades contemporary society and often undermines community identity; rapid structural changes; globalization of the economy; the widening gap between the rich and the poor; massive migration; the marginalization of Christian faith; and the broadening of the scope of educational functions, which are becoming ever more specialized.[6] And, of course, from our own experience we are quite aware of many more challenges.

As far back as 1979, *Catechesi Tradendae* stated that, if there is no community of faith and Christian life, catechesis runs the risk of becoming barren. The document then speaks of the responsibility of the ecclesial community to provide such an environment.[7] There is a section in the document *The Catholic School on the Threshold of the Third Millenium* that emphasizes the ecclesial nature of the Catholic school. It is worth quoting in full:

> The ecclesial nature of the Catholic school . . . is written in the very heart of its identity as a teaching institution. It is a true and proper ecclesial entity by reason of its educational activity, "in which faith, culture and life are brought into harmony." Thus it must be strongly empha-sized that this ecclesial dimension is not a mere adjunct, but is a proper and specific attribute, a distinctive char-acteristic which penetrates and informs every moment of its educational activity, a fundamental part of its very identity and the focus of its mission. The fostering of this dimension should be the aim of all those who make up the educating community.[8]

Here we clearly see the idea of the community of the school at the heart of the community of the Church. The school is a place of ecclesial experience, molded within the Christian community. The task of living and communicating the spirituality of com-munion within the school community derives from the school's being by its very nature a part of the Church communion.[9]

Earlier, *Consecrated Persons* speaks of the need for an "atmo-sphere characterized by a search for truth in which competent,

[6] TM introduction.
[7] CT 24.
[8] TM 11.
[9] CP 42.

convinced and coherent educators, teachers of learning and
of life, may be a reflection, albeit imperfect but still vivid, of
the one Teacher."[10] This reminds us that we are a community
bound together as we carry out our task. The educating community "is constituted by the interaction and collaboration
of its various components: students, parents, teachers, direc-
tors and nonteaching staff. Attention is rightly given to the
importance of relations existing among all who make up the
educating community."[11] There then comes a very significant
statement we would do well to bear in mind: we are reminded
that this community dimension in the Catholic school is not
a merely *sociological* category; it has a *theological* foundation
as well. The primary responsibility for creating this unique
Christian school climate rests with the teachers as individuals
and as a community.[12]

The climate of the school and the commitment of the teacher
are emphasized: it is essential that each member of the school
community adopts a common vision, a common outlook on
life, based on adherence to the scale of values in which he or
she believes.[13] These values are communicated through the
interpersonal and sincere relationships of its members.[14] All
of this is done in a community where, for Christians, Christ is
naturally the foundation of the whole educational enterprise.[15]

The document *Lay Catholics in the Schools* notes that when
teachers contribute their initiative, their creativity, and their
competent, conscious, and enthusiastic labor to the task, the
whole people of God will be able to distinguish Gospel values
being lived by these teachers who are witnesses to the faith.[16]

[10] CP 14.
[11] CP 18.
[12] CP 19.
[13] CS 29.
[14] CS 32.
[15] CS 34.
[16] LC 10.

Everything the teacher does in the school is situated within what ought to be an educational community. As members of the educational community, these educators influence, and are influenced by, the social ambience of the school. Therefore, close relationships should be established with one's colleagues and also with other groups that make us into an educational community.[17] Our task is to foster the transition from the school as an institution to the school as a community.[18]

I have identified two specific outcomes that result from living in the Catholic school as a community. The first of these is the necessity of working at the spreading of the Gospel, the Good News or *kerygma*, something that is our mission and, ultimately, God's own mission. The other necessary outcome is the development of the whole human person.

When discussing the meaning of *koinonia* earlier, I noted that when people live in deep communion with one another, there is always a need for outreach. People become eager to share the faith, to hand it on to others. And this holds not only in the spiritual dimension. There is always an impulse to reach out in practical charity. The Catholic school forms part of the saving mission of the Church[19] and, since Christ is the foundation of the whole educational enterprise in a Catholic school, his revelation gives new meaning to life and helps all people to make the Beatitudes the norm of life. In fact, "the Catholic school finds its true justification in the mission of the Church; it is based on an educational philosophy in which faith, culture, and life are brought into harmony. Through it the local Church evangelizes, educates, and contributes to the formation of a healthy and morally sound lifestyle among the members."[20]

Since the call to personal holiness and to apostolic mission is common to all people, teachers must be ready to proclaim

[17] LC 34.
[18] RD 31.
[19] CS 9.
[20] RD 34.

the message through their words and witness to it in what they do. They are to work for the sanctification of the world from within, in the manner of leaven, and make Christ known to others.[21]

This call to mission is expressed very strongly in many of the documents, and I think the call applies to everyone who shares in the life of Christ. It is a call to be witnesses to Christ, an epiphany of the love of God in the world, a call for us to become recognizable signs of a reconciled humanity. We have to "live the present as *kairós,* a favorable time, so that the Gospel may effectively reach the men and women of today."[22] It is a prophetic task of *"recalling and serving the divine plan for humanity,* as it is announced in Scripture and as also emerges from the attentive reading of the signs of God's providential action in history."[23] It is a task that "requires the courage of testimony and the patience of dialogue."[24] Each Catholic school and each person within it are called to show the face of God's love to the world.

Concern for the human person is an outcome of the depth of the community in the school. In *Consecrated Persons* we read: "A school's community dimension is inseparable from priority attention to the person, the focus of the scholastic educational person. . . . The humanism which we desire advocates a vision of society centered on the human person and his inalienable rights, on the values of justice and peace, on a correct relationship between individuals, society and the State, on the logic of solidarity and subsidiarity."[25] And soon after: "Each pupil must be considered as an individual, bearing in mind his family environment, his personal history, his

[21] LC 7.
[22] CP 2.
[23] CP 2.
[24] CP 2.
[25] CP 60.

skills and interests."[26] It is imperative for us, in other words, to create and work in a climate of trust in our schools.

This same document issues a very great challenge: to a strongly standardized and individualistic society we have to propose an alternative model of human coexistence. We must undertake to ensure that schools are structured as places of encounter, listening, and communication, where students experience fundamental values in an essential way. There must be pedagogical choices that promote an overcoming of individualistic self-promotion, that foster solidarity instead of competition, assistance of the weak instead of their marginalization, responsible participation instead of indifference.[27] "Community life, when interwoven out of deep relationships, itself becomes prophetic in a society which sometimes without realizing it has a profound yearning for [brotherhood] which knows no borders. This conviction becomes visible in the commitment to make the life of the community a place of growth of persons and of mutual aid in the search and fulfillment of the common mission."[28] Such a community both educates and forms the human person. A synthesis occurs between culture and faith.

The Catholic school must, indeed, set out to be a school *for* the human person and *of* human persons. The focus ought to be on the human person in his or her integral, transcendent, and historical identity.[29] Only in an environment where the school is truly a community can values be communicated through the sincere and interpersonal relationships of its members. In such an environment, learning is facilitated when the educational interaction is at a level that fully recognizes the equality and dignity of every human person.[30]

[26] CP 61.
[27] CP 46.
[28] CP 48.
[29] TM 9.
[30] CP 45.

When such respect for human persons truly obtains within the school community, inclusiveness and love will also pervade the atmosphere. One section of the *Third Millenium* document has the heading "Care for Learning Means Loving." Here we read: "In its ecclesial dimension another characteristic of the Catholic school is that it is a school for all, with special attention to those who are weakest." The text then goes on to speak of the "new poor," those to whom no values are proposed, those who do not know the beauty of the faith, who come from families that are broken and incapable of love, often living as well in material and spiritual poverty: "To these new poor the Catholic School turns in a spirit of love."[31]

This is the challenge: to show love. "Teachers love their students, and they show this love in the way they interact with them. They take advantage of every opportunity to encourage and strengthen them in those areas which will help them to achieve the goals of the educational process. Their words, their witness, their encouragement and help, their advice and friendly correction are all important in achieving these goals which must always be understood to include academic achievement, moral behavior and a religious dimension."[32]

The question of intercultural education is raised in terms of its being a sign of richness and a promise of growth.[33] It is also noted that at times, diversity between cultures is often a source of misunderstandings and conflicts. We see at times how some cultures establish themselves arrogantly over others. This completely contradicts the fact that we believe in the value of each human person. This document uses a useful phrase—*coexistence of differences*—which could apply to other than just cultural differences.[34] If we can reach across our differences and embrace everyone, we may become a sign of the vastness

[31] TM 15.
[32] RD 110.
[33] CP 66.
[34] CP 67.

of God. Timothy Radcliffe, the former master general of the Dominicans, once said that communities of the like-minded are but weak signs of the kingdom. Thus our challenge is to hold each human person in acceptance and love, whatever his or her strengths or weaknesses.

3. *Communio*: A Benedictine Gift

My comments about communion in the Benedictine tradition can be grouped under these headings:

- some general comments about living in communion,
- the spread of the good news about this, and
- the importance that Benedict places on the human person.

a) Benedict and Community

Benedictine life has been called a "school of communion"—a school where we live in communion with one another and keep on learning to do so. There is no doubt that communion is the reality at the heart of Benedictine life. Communion with God is expressed or incarnated in communion with our brothers and sisters; in fact, we could also broaden that communion to say that we must live in communion with other cultures, other faiths, even with the planet.

It is interesting that Benedict uses the word *communio* rarely (only 3 times, in 38.2, 10; 63.4), and that only when he is talking about sacramental Holy Communion, though he does use the word *communis* to refer to the common rule of the monastery, the common possession of all, and the common table (7.55; 33.6; 43.15). The word he chooses to describe community is *congregatio,* and this is used twenty-five times. Thus is apparent Benedict's suggestion of the community as the Lord's flock, a pastoral and relational image. This includes both the idea of a vertical relationship with God and of horizontal relationships with one another. This is absolutely central in the Rule: we are called into community by God—"Is there

anybody here who yearns for life?" (Prol. 14). It is by God's life
that we live. We are already established in this relationship by
baptism. We live in the divine presence (19.1) and at all times
live in mindfulness of God; we keep him in mind, always remember him, never forget him (7.10). Nor is there any doubt in
the Rule about the great importance of our relationships with
one another. The word *frater* ("brother") is used ninety-three
times, and there is significant use of the word *invicem* ("one
another") (ten times). Benedict's word for "together" *(pariter)*
is used only four times, but its final usage in chapter 72.12 is
powerful. We pray that Christ, to whom we prefer absolutely
nothing, will bring us *all together* to everlasting life.

I could never stress enough my conviction concerning the
relational anthropology of the Rule. This foundation is at the
heart of our communal living and working together. Within
the community, a veritable web of relationships, we can create
a sacred space where all can discover their own uniqueness
and giftedness. It is the locus where we learn to discover God's
presence in every aspect and dimension of our lives; and then
this vision impels us to go out of ourselves to serve others.
In this place we work toward the transformation and growth
of each member, and simultaneously toward the growth and
transformation of relationships, which constitute the actual
life of the community.

In Benedict's definition of the four kinds of monks, the
cenobites are those who live in community and belong to a
monastery, where they serve under a rule and an abbot (1.2).
Benedict thus presumes that monks ought to have a way of
life to guide them, in a specific place and with a specific leader.
As persons shaped by this way of life, they make three promises: *stability* in this particular place and community, *fidelity* to
this way of life *(conversatio morum)*, and *obedience* to the abbot
(58.17). Mutual obedience—that is, listening to one another
effectively—is also part of the way of life. Conversely, Benedict
also shows what is valuable in this communion by condemning those who do not live as they should, in particular the

sarabaites who live without a rule and do as they like, and the gyrovagues who never settle down and are slaves to their own will (1.6-11).

b) The "Good News" Is Proclaimed by Our Very Life and Actions

One of the most important things Benedict proclaims in his Rule is the centrality of Christ for those who live this way of life. No fewer than twenty times does Benedict refer to Christ. Thus, from the very beginning of the Prologue (where we are urged to take up the weapons of obedience and do battle for the true King, Christ the Lord, Prol. 3), straight through to the last chapter (where we are reminded that we need to keep this little rule for beginners with Christ's help as we make the journey to our heavenly home, 73.8), Christ is clearly the reason for our living. Let me remind you of some of Benedict's very familiar phrases.

We see Christ in the abbot, who holds the place of Christ in the monastery (2.2). He is the one who makes Christ present to the community. We see Christ in the sick ("Care of the sick must rank above and before all else, so that they may truly be served as Christ," [36.1]), in the guests ("All guests who present themselves are to be welcomed as Christ, . . . and in them Christ is to be adored," [53.1, 6]). We are to "prefer nothing to the love of Christ" (4.21) and, even more emphatically, "Let them prefer nothing whatever to Christ" (72.11). It is Christ who enables us to forgive and be reconciled (4.72) and who enables us to fulfill our commitments even with ease. Through perfect love of God, which is reached after the long journey toward humility, the monk "will now begin to observe without effort, as though naturally, from habit, no longer out of fear of hell, but out of love for Christ, good habit and delight in virtue" (7.69).

It seems obvious that the experience of a life of prayer as described in detail in chapters 8–20 and in chapter 52 is something that enables the monk to fulfill the inherent obligations of living in community. This is something the community does together, and eagerness for the Work of God on the part of a candidate is, in fact, one of the criteria that shows whether one who wishes to enter the community is truly seeking God (58.7).

"Service in love" could be the synonym for monastic work. The word "service" is repeated several times in the description of how the monks are to carry out their work in the kitchen and at meals. Except for those engaged in other important community duties, all are to participate in such service. First Benedict says they are to "serve one another," and then a few verses later he says that this service is to be done "in love" (35.1, 6). Every care is to be taken to enable this service to be done well. Help is to be given to the servers if needed, and the ones serving are to be given concessions such as extra food and drink so that they may carry out the service willingly.

Several chapters of the Rule are devoted to the central symbol of the *table*. Like the eucharistic table, the table of the community's meals is a symbol of unity, service, and love. This symbol appears in a reverse kind of way in the chapters on excommunication, where we find that those who commit faults against the community are to be excluded from the table and given time to reflect on their failures and so be healed (chaps. 23–30). If the fault is less serious, the exclusion happens from the table only. If it is more serious, it is from the table and the oratory as well, so that the erring monk cannot participate in the common prayer or the common table. I will refer in the next section to the processes of forgiveness and reconciliation that illustrate the care for the monk who has been excluded. At the table, generosity of provisions is emphasized: not only is bread provided, but a *generous* pound of bread is offered. As I said, it is easy to draw comparisons between a theology of the table for meals and the theology of the table of the Eucharist, where all are bound together in sharing and experiencing God's lavish love.

Two major elements that are destructive of communal living receive stern treatment by Benedict, and this makes one think of the conversely positive side presented in a united community. In Benedict's mind it would be good news to have members of his community able to share all, since he so resoundingly condemns the vice of private ownership. To this purpose he quotes the texts from Acts, "all things should be the common possession of all" (Acts 4:32), and the opposite behavior is called a vice which must be torn out by the roots (33.1). A community that truly shares everything is one that proclaims the good news that the seeking of God is more important than the possession of material things.

The second dangerous element to communal living is the evil of murmuring or grumbling. Everything must be done to prevent this insidious practice from destroying the community. Murmuring is one of the faults condemned in the chapters that speak of exclusion for faults (23.1). The monk should not even murmur in his heart (5.17). All is to be done in the community to prevent even justifiable murmuring (41.5). Rowan Williams once asked, "What is the currency in the community?" If the currency is one of murmuring and discontent, a united community will not thrive, nor will it be able to witness to unity and love.

c) Concern for the Human Person

One would probably have to survey the whole of Benedict's Rule to cover this aspect which appears so frequently in the text, and so here I can only mention a few examples briefly.

Perhaps the most obvious reference to "concern for the human person" is the care given to individual needs. Account is to be taken of individual needs, and here Benedict uses another text from the Acts passage we have quoted: "Distribution was made to each one as he had need" (Acts 4:35; RB 34.1). This is to be done in consideration for weaknesses. Two kinds of cooked food are to be provided at table because of individual weaknesses. In this way the person who may not be able to eat one kind of food may partake of the other (39.2-3). In fact, if fruit or vegetables are available there can be a third dish. In the event that local conditions generate extra work or impose summer heat, a greater amount of drink may be provided (40.5). Those who are engaged in important business are to be excused from kitchen service, as is the cellarer if the community is large (35.5). Clothing is to be fitted to the wearer (55.8) and adapted according to climate (55.1). It is noteworthy in all these texts that care of individuals is to be expressed in such ordinary things as food, drink, and clothing. There is nothing esoteric about such care; it concerns practical and daily things that are very ordinary. Those who are sick are to be cared for by someone who is God-fearing, and the abbot should consider the sick one of his prime concerns (36).

When needed, help is to be given to officials, for example the cellarer: "If the community is rather large he should be given helpers that with their assistance he may calmly perform the duties of office" (31.17). Additional help is to be given to those in the kitchen of the guests when needed (53.17), and the porter is to be given the help of a younger brother if he needs help (66.5).

Perhaps the most significant example of care for the individual is the concern that is shown concerning the erring brother—what happens when he errs, and how he is able to be forgiven. Such a brother is sometimes noted as being "sick," sometimes as "wavering," and sometimes as "delinquent," but at all times he is still called "brother." Having excluded him from the table, or both the table and the oratory, the abbot is to show great solicitude for him and to be careful that he is not overwhelmed with too great a burden of sorrow. The abbot himself may not be the most appropriate person to go and give him comfort, and in that case he should send wise elders to show the erring brother compassion. In the end, the abbot has to be both physician and good shepherd, and he must go to seek out the lost and carry him back (27.9).

The rituals marking the erring brother's return to the community are spelled out in chapter 44, where the brother who has been outside the community is taken back after he has reflected on his mistakes and is prepared to go through a

process of gradual reintegration. Forgiveness and reconciliation are key issues in the community. All members are urged
to make peace before the setting of the sun, and enemies are
to be prayed for in the love of Christ. The culmination of all
these injunctions is that we are never to despair of the mercy
of God (4.72-74).

The abbot is obviously the one who holds authority in the
community, and we can draw on many examples of how he
is to act with concern for those who are his responsibility. In
his *Commentary on Saint John's Gospel*, Saint Thomas Aquinas
says that the leader of the community must show two things
toward those he leads: he is to be responsible for them and
he is to love them. One of these is not enough without the
other, he says. These two attitudes are reflected in chapters
2 and 24. The abbot is certainly responsible for his community and accountable for them (2.7, 34; 64.7), but he also has
to take account of the different temperaments present: "He
may have to threaten or coax by turns and be at times stern
as a taskmaster and at others devoted and tender as only a
father can be. With the undisciplined and restless he will use
firm argument; with the obedient and docile and patient he
will use appeal for greater virtue; but as for the negligent and
disdainful, we charge him to use reproof and rebuke" (2.25).
For the abbot, it should be more important to be loved than to
be feared (64.15). Even when punishing, he will not crush the
bruised reed nor break the vessel by rubbing too hard (64.12-
13), and he has to arrange everything so that "the strong have
something to yearn for and the weak nothing to run from"
(64.19). He must also listen to the wisdom of the community,
believing that each person, and especially the young, must
contribute to the common welfare (chap. 3).

Chapter 72 contains a key message of the Rule, a message of
love which covers all we have said about the human person. If
we live the good zeal we will live in respect for others, we will
be able to support their weaknesses. We will wholeheartedly
consider and listen to the others, and promotion of self will

not be the aim of our lives. Furthermore, love of those who lead us, of one another, and of God will be the operative and evident force within the community.

In fact, the general principle that best shows the urgency of exercising great concern for all is "that the abbot is to regulate and arrange all matters that souls may be saved and the brothers may go about their activities without justifiable grumbling" (40.5). In this way, peace will reign.

4. Implications

What conclusions, then, are we to draw from both the documents and the teaching of the Rule in our educational endeavors, in the context of schools that are both Catholic and Benedictine? How do we show that this is what we are? What will inspire us as we move into the future?

I hope readers have been able to relate the points I have made to their own concrete circumstances as I have raised them throughout this chapter. But now I would like to attempt a brief summary of my own. I believe that both the documents of the Church on education and the Rule of Saint Benedict call us to the following tasks as we move into the future. And I make these points as a suggestion for a serious *renewal of our commitment* in the present, since it goes without saying that we have already been striving to give our lives wholeheartedly to this enterprise!

a) We Are Called to Proclaim the Gospel Message in Word and in Deed

- Hence our schools must provide an environment which both encourages and makes this possible.
- We must remember that the education and formation of all concerned are necessary.
- We know that to build a community that lives and proclaims the Gospel requires effort and prayer.

- We need strong leadership that listens, helps to form and express a vision, and enables us to keep the vision alive as we struggle to live it.

b) In Whatever We Do, the Development of the Human Person Must Be at the Center

- The development of the students to their full potential, both in their life of faith and in their cultural life, is crucial.
- As part of this challenge, leaders must both challenge and inspire and also be themselves cared for.
- Mutual and collaborative attitudes must be maintained among staff members and with all who are part of the process: parents, boards, Church, and government authorities.
- Relationships need to be warm and loving.

c) There Must Be Inclusiveness for All, Especially the Needy

- We need to establish ways by which those differences and tensions which will inevitably arise can be forgiven, and unity restored.
- We need to develop rituals through which this can be achieved.
- We must find ways of operating that will be inclusive of all.

d) Finally, We Need to Value What We Do and Proclaim That It Is Good

- We have given ourselves for the spread of the reign of God.
- We must maintain real hope that what we do, with God's help, is very much worthwhile.
- If we can do all that we have been considering, we will be providing what the world needs so much: stable, loving, and peaceful arenas.

In her book *The Spirituality of Community*, the American writer Adele Gonzales gives us a word from Teilhard de Chardin that ought to go on resonating in our hearts and minds long after this book has been closed: "Love alone can unite living beings so as to complete and fulfill them, . . . for it alone joins them by what is deepest in themselves. All we need is to imagine our ability to love developing, until it embraces the totality of people and the earth."[35]

[35] Adele Gonzales, *The Spirituality of Community* (Maryknoll, NY: Orbis Books, 2009), 122.

Epilogue

A Gift for the Future

THIS IS A COLLECTION OF ESSAYS WRITTEN over a span of more than a decade. Most of them were written in response to a request for a paper at a conference or seminar and then later prepared for publication. Some arose out of an interest at a particular time when preparing material for a lecture or a retreat. All of them come from a desire to explore more deeply some aspects of the Rule of Saint Benedict, especially as it can apply to our lives today. More and more in my work, I see that so many principles of the Rule can be helpful for all who are trying to live faithfully in whatever way of life they feel called to follow. So the Rule is indeed a gift for all of us, both for the present and the future.

The practical way in which these essays emerged has at least two implications. First, they do not address every aspect of the Rule—it was never intended that they do this. Then, too, some repetition is inevitable: similar themes, ideas, and expressions appear in varying contexts. To me this indicates the importance of such ideas in the Rule.

Some of the essays deal with general aspects of Benedictine life that are central: for instance, what is required of those who live in what Benedict calls "the house of God," the sacramental aspects of that life, asceticism, and obedience.

Another group of essays deals with questions relating to authority: authority as a service of love, the influence of Augustine on Benedict's teaching on the abbot, and the involvement of the whole community by the taking of counsel.

171

Yet a third group discusses our prayer and liturgical life: listening and prayer, the Work of God, Lent and Easter, and the symbol of the table and the Eucharist.

Many other important aspects of Benedictine communal life recur and are emphasized frequently from different angles: the central place of Christ, service of one another, reconciliation, and forgiveness.

If we are to think of the Rule of Saint Benedict as a gift for the future, it is essential that aspects of adaptation be addressed. This is nothing new, as the Rule has been adapted in many ways over the centuries by those who live the way of life in different eras and places. But perhaps something that is peculiarly new in our present times is the growing realization that the Rule can offer much to help all who are seeking God in many and varied ways of life. I think the Rule can offer this because of Benedict's flexibility, his awareness of individual needs, and the balance and moderation that he made the trademark of the Rule.

Two of the essays reflect this. The essay on "Timeless Principles and Contemporary Realities" illustrates how an English Benedictine monk, John Bede Polding, was able to establish my own community, the Sisters of the Good Samaritan of the Order of Saint Benedict, adapting the Rule to the vastly different circumstances of Australia and the needs of this new colony in 1857. Core elements of the Rule were to be maintained, but other elements were also introduced that enabled the sisters to respond to the needs of the time without the constraints that strict enclosure demanded. Perhaps it is only from the perspective of more than a century and a half later that we can see just how radical this adaptation was.

In our current climate there is a call for wider adaptation in a situation where ministries that once were carried out mainly by religious are now shared widely by many people who are not vowed religious. The grace and value of Benedictine life is now embraced by many who share these ministries, something that becomes evident in the final essay that speaks of *communio* and how it can influence those who work in schools that are connected with Benedictine religious. This could also apply to various other ministries.

There are many committed and faithful people in all walks of life who are helped by the Rule of Saint Benedict as they truly seek God. They may not live in a "house of God" in the way that professed religious do, but the world of all of us together can be a house of God. So, indeed, the Rule provides a way of life that is a gift for the future.

Sources

Permission was granted to reprint from the following articles. All rights reserved.

Malone, Margaret. "An Adventure Tale of Divine Love." Address at the meeting of American Benedictine Prioresses, Nassau, Bahamas, January–February, 2002. *Benedictines* 56, no. 2 (fall/winter 2003).

———. "Authority—A Service of Love." *Tjurunga* 69 (November, 2005).

———. "Benedictine Life—A Sacramental Life." Address at the meeting of the Benedictine Union held at New Norcia Abbey, Western Australia, 2007. *Tjurunga* 74 (May, 2008).

———. "Benedictine Tradition—Timeless and Contemporary." *Tjurunga* 72 (May, 2007).

———. "Benedict's Abbot and Saint Augustine." Paper given at the Patristics Conference, Oxford, 1995. *Tjurunga* 53 (1997).

———. "*Communio*: The Church and the Benedictine School." Paper given at the Benedictine Education Conference, Munich, November, 2010. *Tjurunga* 79 (November, 2010).

———. "Community, Table and Eucharist." *Tjurunga* 65 (December, 2003).

———. "Lay Aside Everything." *Tjurunga* 67 (November, 2004).

———. "Listening with the Heart." On-line Paulist Journal (2005).

———. "Living in the House of God." *Tjurunga* 75 (November, 2008).

———. "Looking Forward to Holy Easter." *Tjurunga* 60 (May, 2001).

———. "Obedience—A Listening Stance." Paper given at the meeting of American Benedictine Prioresses, Nassau, Bahamas, 2002.

———. "Seek Peace and Pursue It." Paper given at the meeting of Communio Internationalis Benedictinarum, Sydney, Australia, September, 2003. *Tjurunga* 66 (May, 2004).

———. "Taking Counsel—A Search for Wisdom." *Tjurunga* 67 (November, 2004).